media
MANUAL

RECEIVED

D0345731

**Creating Special Effects
for TV and Video**

CANCELLED 1 9 JUL 2022

m
media
MANUAL

Creating Special Effects for TV and Video

Third Edition

Bernard Wilkie

Focal Press

OXFORD AMSTERDAM BOSTON LONDON NEW YORK PARIS
SAN DIEGO SAN FRANCISCO SINGAPORE SYDNEY TOKYO

Focal Press
An imprint of Elsevier Science
Linacre House, Jordan Hill, Oxford OX2 8DP
200 Wheeler Road, Burlington MA 01803

First published 1977
Reprinted 1978, 1982, 1983, 1986, 1987, 1990
Second edition 1991
Reprinted 1993, 1994
Third edition 1996
Reprinted 1997, 2000
Transferred to digital printing 2003

British Library Cataloguing in Publication Data
A catalogue record for this book is available from the British Library

Library of Congress Cataloguing in Publication Data
A catalogue record for this book is available from the Library of Congress

ISBN 0 240 51474 2

For information on all Focal Press publications
visit our website at www.focalpress.com

Contents

7

8

Introduction

The growth of computer-generated special effects has led some people to believe that most television visual effects will eventually be created electronically. The argument for this is a powerful one based on the fact that the computer with its facility to memorise images – coupled with the support of software which can bend shapes, alter textures and change lighting angles – could be used to input stored effects into any relevant programme: it is easy to see the possibilities.

Nevertheless, there will always be 'horses for courses' and while the tail of a gaseous comet hurtling through space would be best achieved as a computer-generated animation, other, more physical, effects will continue to be produced in the workshop.

In this third edition of *Creating Special Effects* I have up-dated the section on the computer, but it is a highly complex subject and anyone needing more detailed information should refer to the Further Reading on p 180.

Some traditional techniques have also been upgraded to include new methods and materials and these have been published in the appropriate sections: I hope readers will find the results useful.

Bernard Wilkie

Safety Warning

THIS BOOK IS INTENDED AS A GUIDE FOR THOSE PEOPLE WHOSE TASK IT IS TO PROVIDE SPECIAL EFFECTS FOR TELEVISION AND VIDEO. MANY OF THE MATERIALS, PROCESSES AND TECHNIQUES DESCRIBED COULD BE DANGEROUS WHEN USED BY INEXPERIENCED PERSONNEL OR IN UNTRIED OR UNTESTED CONDITIONS.

THE RESPONSIBILITY FOR THEIR USE MUST BE VESTED IN THE USER: THE AUTHOR HAS DONE NO MORE THAN SET DOWN PRACTICES, MATERIALS AND TECHNIQUES WHICH ARE IN USE THROUGHOUT THE INDUSTRY.

MORE DETAILED INFORMATION CAN BE FOUND IN *THE TECHNIQUE OF SPECIAL EFFECTS IN TELEVISION* BY THE SAME AUTHOR.

Special Effects Design

Television viewers and movie-goers watching a battle scene know that it has been especially staged for their benefit. They realise that the shell bursts are planted and that the victims are played by stunt artistes. But what they don't know, and shouldn't know, is that elsewhere in programmes are dozens of 'special effects' designed to make the most ordinary things behave in extraordinary ways.

Diverse and often complex, these unseen effects can range from the breaking of a cup to a vehicle overturning on a bend.

In real life such things happen accidentally; in TV and movies they have to occur on cue and in the right place. Every detail must be pre-ordained and under control.

The special effects designer

An effects designer must have several essential skills as well as a wide-ranging knowledge of crafts, trades and techniques. The most versatile designers are those who are as much at home with an arc welder as they are with an artist's brush. A designer who can create sculptures, paint pictures and design jewellery should also be able to mould fibreglass, build walls and wire an electric circuit. There are few limits, if any, to the requirements of the script or the call on a designer's ability to deal with them.

Overlapping responsibility

It would be impractical for any effects designer, however skilled, to tackle every requirement. Therefore certain elements of the work, such as stunts, make-up, costumes and lighting, are handled by other specialists, the effects designer playing the role of creative co-ordinator.

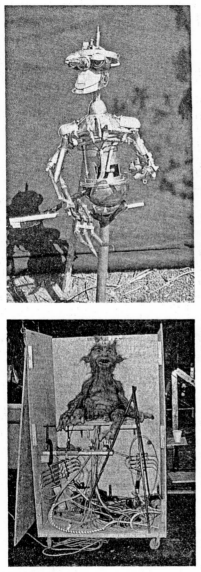

Imagination

Imagination is the key to good special effects. Any competent craftsperson can make things, but it's knowing what to make that is so important. The designer who, with one magic idea, can solve an insoluble problem, is worth more to the production than any amount of re-writing or re-shooting. Special effects are as much about saving time and money as they are about creating drama and fantasy.

The Importance of Sound

In this business it isn't always what the viewers see so much as what they believe they see. An actor swinging a punch at another actor's face will deliberately miss, knowing that a sound effect of knuckles striking flesh will be dubbed on to the sound-track.

Manipulated sound plays a most important part in special effects, and the effects designer should consider its use when planning a sequence.

The restaurant

Picture a scene in a restaurant where two people are dining. What the viewer sees is a table appointed with silver cutlery and elegant candles. A waiter enters, hands the pair a menu and, later, takes their order. We know that we're in a busy restaurant because, although we see only this bit of it, we can hear a hubbub of conversation and a clatter of knives and forks; from across the unseen room a woman laughs.

But this restaurant doesn't exist. Outside the frame there is nothing but studio. We have been purposely misled.

Obviously no director would be happy to record a long sequence in such a small set, but for a brief establishing shot it would serve perfectly well. The designer, assisted by sound, would have created an entire restaurant in a few square feet.

The battle

In the same fashion we can create a battle scene. This, too, can be quite small – a fox-hole sheltering a couple of soldiers. The occasional flare or nearby explosion illuminates the scene as the two men keep their heads down. The sounds of battle are all around. We hear the whine of a passing shell and the rat-tat-tat of a far-off machine-gun. Suddenly there is a flash, brighter than all the rest, accompanied by a frightening bang. The soldiers press themselves into the ground as earth and stones ricochet into the fox-hole. Seconds later smoke drifts across the picture. The tension is almost unbearable as we share the plight of the unfortunate men trapped in that small space.

But what actually happened? Apart from the occasional flashing of the electrician's scissors*, a short use of the smoke machine and the few handfuls of peat flung into the set, our battle existed entirely on audio tape.

---

*A scissor-like device holding two carbon rods which is used to create a brilliant electric arc (page 176).

The Camcorder

The home video camera is proving to be a useful tool for the professional. Able to provide instant moving pictures without involving studio equipment it has become a boon to designers, assistant directors and many others engaged in television and movie production. It is used to record location details, rehearsal routines and action continuity.

The camcorder is particularly useful in the field of special effects, where it is used to assess and analyse workshop experiments and pre-rehearsals. It can also be used to show directors and producers what they may expect in the final recording and to familiarise actors with effects sequences in which they will be taking part.

Transitory effects
Many effects are short-lived and difficult to evaluate by eye. Explosions and bullet effects sometimes fall into this category. The camcorder can prove invaluable (particularly on location) in assessing the best means of deployment. There is little point in arranging a dramatic run of bullet hits if the furthest ones will be obscured by dust from the ones in front.

Filmed sequences
35 and 16mm film cameras continue to be widely used in movie and television production. This can make life difficult for the special effects designer who has no means of knowing positively what is 'in the can'. Rushes shown the following day could reveal unacceptable blunders.

To get round this problem it is now common practice to operate a small camcorder alongside the main film camera. Results can be viewed instantly and faults rectified before the set is dismantled and the artists released.

One important thing to remember is that the camcorder will record the scene at a slightly different angle from that of the film camera. This should be allowed for and doubts expelled by re-checking through the viewfinder of the main camera. (No! That hand will not have been in shot on the film.)

The camcorder, although useful for tests of this nature, should never be used to assess the quality of studio lighting, the colours of costumes or the suitability of make-up.

Film Cameras

Although video cameras can now be made to record at varying speeds it is usual to employ film cameras for professional high and low speed requirements.

Many effects benefit from being slowed down or speeded up. For example, if a man falls from a roof top the action appears more effective if his fall occupies more time than it would at normal speed. This also applies to some explosions which become apparently more powerful when slowed down. Alternatively, some sequences benefit from being speeded up, such as the action of a gunslinger going for his Colt. Automobile crashes are nearly always enhanced by this technique when the action is in close up. In long-shot when they career over cliff-tops, they need to be slowed down of course.

Camera speeds

A high filming speed is used to slow down the action when projected. A slow filming speed is used to speed things up. There are, of course, limits to the speeds, both slow and fast, to which cameras can be run. Where very high speeds are required, special equipment must be obtained. Nevertheless most 16mm and 35mm cameras are capable of being run at speeds slower and faster than normal.

High speed cameras use a lot of film. Many dozens of feet pass through the gate as the camera motor gets up to speed and many more are wasted as it slows down again.

One problem encountered with high speed filming is the necessity to provide sufficient light. The faster the speed the more light is required and this often implies that the lights have to be positioned very close to the subject.

Stop-frame and time-lapse camera

Single-frame cameras used for cartoon and animation work are invariably custom-built for their particular purposes. Ordinary cameras designed for normal running may not hold each frame sufficiently steady to prevent the completed film from showing obvious signs of 'hunting'.

Stop-frame cameras are usually operated remotely by solenoid and cable to avoid camera movement. Exposures with time-lapse cameras are invariably controlled by a time switch set to operate the shutter at pre-determined intervals. The timing device is also used to switch on the lights prior to a take and to switch them off afterwards. It is important to allow sufficient time for the lamps to warm up if the resultant film is to be flicker-free.

Explosions

Small explosions will look bigger if they are filmed at a slightly higher speed.

Falls

Dramatic sequences such as men falling from buildings can often benefit from prolonged motion. These call for the high speed camera.

Car chase

A car chase in which the driver must negotiate tricky or hazardous obstacles looks more impressive if the action is speeded up. This requires a slow speed camera.

Fights

Fight sequences are enhanced if the speed of action is increased. This calls for a slowed-down camera.

15

Animation Stand Camerawork

A film camera which records one frame at a time is used in the making of animated cartoons or graphs (or even flat three-dimensional objects such as cigarette packs or chocolates, etc.). This camera has rock-steady movements and uses special film with accurately punched sprocket holes. Mounted on a shakeproof vertical column, the camera is suspended over the animation bench on which sheets of artwork can be filmed while being manipulated via a series of rack-and-pinion controls.

For cartoon animation, drawings painted on clear cel are photographed sequentially, each one being placed over a peg bar to ensure accurate registration.

A virtue of the animation camera is that for long sequences it can be programmed to run automatically, zooming, tracking and holding focus without supervision.

Uses

Supposing, for example, it was required to show the load stresses imparted on a bridge. On the animation bench a photograph or a drawing of the bridge could be overlaid with various cels showing stress patterns while cut-out paper arrows could be moved around and other graphics brought in and removed at will. For a commercial in which, say, wrapped candies slid out of their carton and then, while moving around, shed their wrappers, the animation bench would be an ideal tool.

But again the question arises as to whether certain work can be carried out more effectively on the computer; only close analysis of the requirement and the alternative methods will answer that one.

Preparation

Before undertaking any animation it is usual to draw up a storyboard of the action. This defines not only the action but also the time scale. At 24 frames of film a second, it is a simple matter to calculate what distance any component must travel in a given time. The time is assessed with a stop watch while miming the action on a sheet of paper.

When many separate components are being moved it is advisable to prepare a chart and tick off each item once it has been moved. Without this it is very easy to forget whether a piece has been moved or not.

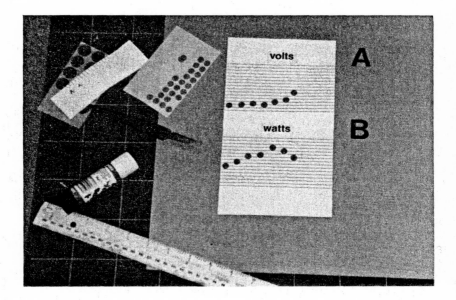

Animation stand camerawork
Graphs and charts: By applying dots or lines to a graph of this kind and filming
each addition at an appropriate interval the results will appear to animate.

Stop-Frame Film Animation

This the technique used in the making of animated puppet films and commercials in which inanimate objects appear to move. Manipulated by hand, the subjects are fractionally re-positioned before each frame of the film is exposed. Computer-generated animation, although now in common use, has not replaced the stop-frame film technique which, to some, has a more pleasing quality.

Technique

Before commencing filming, it is advisable to make a chart of the movements required. Normal film projection is at 24 frames a second and all movement is consequently related to this yardstick.

Each movement is first assessed in real time. Say, for example, that a cigarette pack is required to spin at the rate of one revolution a second. This rotation has to be calculated on the basis that the pack revolves once in 24 separate movements.

In practice, if the movement is too small, it is possible to shoot two or more frames of each position.

Slow movements look realistic, but fast ones often appear jerky.

Puppet construction

Puppets are usually made from flexible material modelled on aluminium wire armatures. They should be 'dead' with no trace of springiness. During animation it should be possible to pin their feet to the baseboard so that one limb is always firmly located. Hours of patient filming can be ruined if a puppet shifts accidently during animation.

Life-sized animation

The animation of full-sized objects is commonplace in the making of certain TV commercials in which people rush around at high speed, food dances on tables and delighted women clean their kitchens in a flash. In the case of inanimate objects it is simply a matter of moving the items, exposing one frame of film, moving them again and so on. But there are things to look out for. In the recording of a long sequence outdoors, the light can change as clouds pass overhead, operators can flatten grass (which causes it to wave violently) and while moving to and fro may inadvertently move something else. Any of these can render hours of work unusable.

Nightmare Spider
With a body of lightweight expanded polystyrene and legs of stiff wire covered in latex and paper tissues, this spider can be animated to move realistically. However, unless the movements or a real spider are studied and copied, the results will look artificial. (This task can be made easier by using a camcorder.)

19

The Computer

Computers, now installed in every modern production suite, are used to guide cameras, record information, produce graphics and control operations. The computer stores information which can be retrieved. It is this facility which makes it so valuable.

As individual chips, 'computers' can be found in electronic equipment where they are used to control simple operations, while at the other end of the scale they can comprise an array of monitors, keyboards, palettes, mice, external links and so on.

Typical of the upper range is the equipment used to create graphics and animations. Requiring none of the usual artists' tools it enables even those who cannot draw to produce elaborate pictures, artwork and printed captions.

In the technical suite there are computer-based devices which when fed with rehearsal data will, during transmission, control the studio lights and monitor camera outputs.

Motion control

For the special-effects designer the choice of techniques has widened considerably. One example is in the use of computer-controlled cameras.

This technique uses computer software to memorise camera movements – including zooms, focusing, panning, tilting and tracking – and to recreate any or all of these functions on command – a substantial improvement on the older methods where the camera operator would be expected to remember and perform all these movements manually. The great advantage of this new system is that it is able to repeat the same movements over and over again with total accuracy and without further human intervention.

Visualise a sequence in which the camera follows the flight of a model aircraft which, in the story, has to be destroyed by an explosive missile in mid-flight. Imagine too that our viewpoint is not from a static camera, but from the attacking aircraft flying behind.

The aircraft would be recorded in a master shot, weaving and jinking to avoid attack. It would then be removed and the camera made to continue its travel. A second pass would include the missile and a third pass would record the explosion through which the camera would fly.

DEATH OF THE MECHANARK.

Episode 5

Long shot: Advancing Mechanark:

C.U.   Lt. Simmins fires blaster.

C.U.   Missile strikes Mechanark in shoulder,
       destroying mechanical arm which detaches
       and falls to ground.

SFX   Please note: Mechanark must not be damaged
       in this take: it is required for Episode 6.

CAMERA   SFX SHOOTING SCRIPT.

1.   Track past Mechanark. Release Arm.
       Record on computer.

2.   Second pass: record missile against black.
       Missile should disappear behind black mask
       representing Mechanark's shoulder.

3   Third pass: Pyrotechnic explosion against black
       in area of shoulder.

Computerised Effects – 1

Although computer-generated stock effects can be employed during recording, computer input is usually reserved for post-production work.

Computer technology has reached a stage where images can be created to mimic real life; the simulation of shining gold or silver letters that turn and twist in the light, their shadows and reflections moving across apparently polished surfaces is a typical example.

Before the computer can create anything it must be given information. This can be input via electronically scanned drawings or photographs, or by the use of models and three-dimensional subjects transmitted from a video camera. Images can also be hand-drawn straight onto the screen via an electronic pen and palette.

The key factor is the software. Using stored information a designer needs only to plot a few points on the screen to create an outline (a 'wire frame') of the required object and use the program to fill in the details. At this stage the object can be given form, e.g. it can be turned from a flat rectangle into a cylinder by lighting it from a particular direction. The program automatically supplies the correct shadows and highlights which make it appear three dimensional.

Explosions
Computer-generated explosions can be tailored to suit the action and moved to any part of the scene. Small explosions can be enlarged and large ones reduced, while the proportion of debris, sparks and brilliance can all be varied. Electronically generated explosions are commonly used in science fiction (combat sequences in spaceships), but pyrotechnic explosions are employed where lingering smoke and practical destruction are required.

Morphing
This is the effect in which one thing apparently turns into another. Given a human face and a lion's head, the computer can be programmed to metamorphose one into the other by a process of interpolation. Key areas such as the nose, mouth and eyes would be given defined parameters and the one face would then transform into the other. Unlike super-imposition, this creates a faultless transition.

Computerised effects – 1
1. Memorised effects can be used to modify other inputs. Here the stored image of corrugated paper is used to texture a stone building.
2. Flames (which far from being 'just flames' are highly complex structures) demonstrate the sort of problems which can confront computer animators.

Computerised Effects – 2

Computer-generated effects offer an alternative to practical ones and should be considered when dangerous or messy sequences are called for.

Flames
It is perfectly feasible to create computer-generated flames, but to achieve authenticity demands time and effort. Real flames break up at their edges, softening and hardening and giving off smoke, factors which can cause problems for the computer operator. It is easier to produce practical flames, but faced with the situation of, say, setting fire to the hair of an elderly actress, a post-production method would seem to be the obvious choice.

Texture
Another way in which computer graphics can aid the designer is in its ability to change textures. Libraries of textural effects, available on disks, can be used to change the surface characteristics of any subject being worked on. For example, a map of an arid desert area could appear to be drawn on sand simply by selecting the appropriate software. A room interior could be given alternative wallpaper and fabric designs in the same way, the various patterns and textures being made to wrap themselves around the contours of the furniture and drapes.

Creativity
One of the most important factors of computer-aided design is that it enables designers to experiment. Prototype effects can be displayed on the monitor and changes made before the sequence is finalised. If it were required to show, for instance, a lava flow it would be an easy matter to use a stock shot or some newsreel footage which could be manipulated to perform anywhere within the picture. Perspective could be created by broadening one end and narrowing the other while flames and hot spots could be enhanced by increasing their brilliance or by adding a separate effect. If the lava had to flow around the contours of a grounded spaceship, the effect could be manipulated to flow along a path contained within specified boundaries. The alternative approach, to record the sequence as a miniature, might prove too daunting.

Whatever the choice, it would undoubtedly be simpler to experiment on the computer screen than in the workshop using buckets of simulated lava.

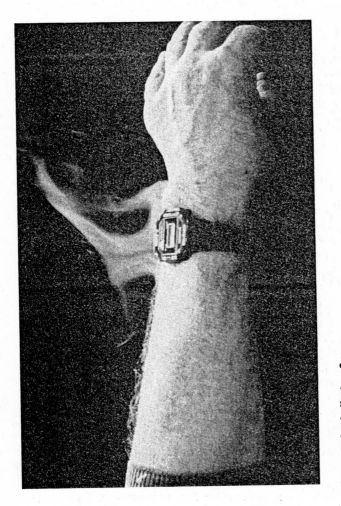

Computerised effects – 2
Faced with the problem of providing a burning wristwatch on a human arm it could be sensible to employ a stored effect programmed to follow the movements of the action. As a technique this can be both expensive and time consuming, but for a short sequence might provide the only practical solution.

25

Fifty-Fifty Mirrors (Beam-Splitters)

Fifty-fifty mirrors are made from optically polished glass coated on one side with a microscopically thin layer of aluminium. The density of coating determines the amount of reflection which, as the term fifty-fifty implies, is designed to return 50 per cent of the light back to source and permitting 50 per cent to pass through.

Ghost effects
With the mirror placed at 45 degrees in front of the camera lens various ghost or super-imposition effects can be achieved.

This technique, while seldom employed in modern television studios, has uses for the camcorder owner needing to combine two pictures with a single camera.

With a 10 centimetre square mirror set in front of the lens, super-imposition of one picture over another can be arranged by simply dimming the light on one while brightening it on the other. An example might be to show a simulated X-ray picture of bones in a human hand using photographs or illustrations. Similarly a real hand and a skeleton hand could be used.

Depth of field
The distance from the lens via the mirror remains as important as it would under normal conditions – i.e. there will be focus problems when attempting to combine distant pictures with close-ups.

For super-imposition effects, it is invariably necessary to use black backgrounds, but they should be kept as far behind the subjects as possible to prevent spilled light causing them to register.

Auto-focus
Videocameras with auto-focus may be fooled into believing that the mirror is the subject. The use of manual focus override will normally deal with this.

One of the benefits of combining two pictures in this fashion is that the results can be seen in the viewfinder or on a monitor at the time of recording.

1. Ghosts and apparitions
A semi-transparent mirror placed at 45° to the camera axis reflects the picture it sees back into the camera lens.

2. Mirrored sparks
An actor presses a switch and is 'electrocuted'. But the sparks, which are produced by touching two electrodes connected to a welding transformer, shower out from a hole in a metal plate and are seen superimposed over the real switch. a, The electrodes. b, Fifty/fifty mirror. c, Wall mounted light switch.

27

Mirrored Effects

It is quite feasible to use conventional mirrors for effects work, but they do have double reflection characteristics that sometimes mar the picture. The effect is often seen where white letters are shown on a black background or where a bright spot of light is seen via a mirror. The front and back surfaces of the glass then throw their own separate reflections. For results that have to be optically perfect, surface-silvered mirrors should be used.

Extending the picture
Mirrors may be used to give added dimensions to small sets, creating the impression that there is far more space than there really is. Large back projection mirrors are sometimes used in this context. A fact that is sometimes overlooked is that there is often more free space between floor and ceiling than between walls of sets. This means that a mirror placed outside a window or porthole can provide a better 'distant vista' than could be obtained by a simple, flat painting. For example, a 'moonscape' built as a model and suspended in a vertical position above the mirror gives a very realistic panorama seen from the window of a 'space-shuttle'.

Changing direction
Mirrors may also be used for changing the direction or position of things without this being apparent on the screen. A ball dropped from the ceiling viewed in a mirror at 45 degrees to the vertical appears to be travelling toward the camera lens along a straight, horizontal path. A model space ship or missile similarly dropped appears to be in level flight (and without the encumbrance of nylon lines or wires).

An alien monster can shoot huge coiled tentacles out toward the viewer with unerring aim when this mirror technique is used.

Calculating reflecting angles
There is a simple method of working out the angles of reflection. It consists of drawing an angle on a piece of paper which is then cut out and laid on a diagram of the arrangement required. For example, to calculate the position and size of mirror for a back projection layout the horizontal angle of the lens must be drawn on paper and cut out as a narrow triangle. Laid over a plan of the screen so that the outer lines touch the edges of the screen the paper can now be folded anywhere along its length to show where the projector may be situated and where the mirror should be. It also shows the angle for the mirror and its horizontal width. This technique may be used for all mirror calculations including the design of periscopes and similar optical devices.

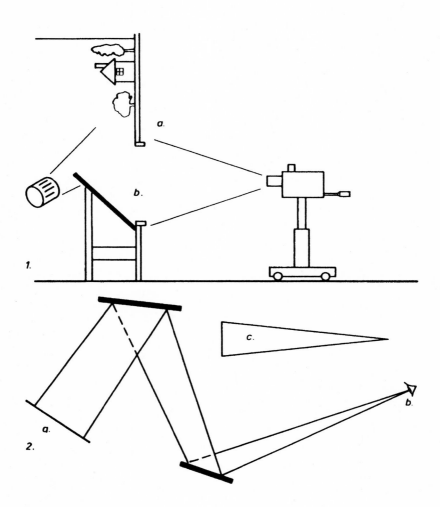

MIRRORED EFFECTS

1. Space saving
Where space is limited, scenes may be extended by using mirrors. In this example a model fastened to the back of a flat (a) appears to be on level ground outside the window (b).

2. Calculating angles
A triangular piece of paper (c) representing the angle-of-view can be folded anywhere along its length to demonstrate the angles of reflection. Folded as shown here it indicates not only the angles of the mirrors but also their sizes to see picture (a) from viewpoint (b).

Periscopes

Mirrors used in the devices outlined below should be surface-silvered on ¼ in polished plate glass. Ordinary mirrors not only give a double image, but the thinner glass distorts when fixed in a frame.

Periscope
Bulky TV and movie cameras can seldom be mounted low enough to obtain a 'worm's-eye view'. For this sort of shot a periscope must be used. Mounted in front of the lens it can lower the apparent viewpoint to a few inches above floor level. Clamped firmly to the camera it can be moved around to give a variety of tracking, panning and even zoom shots. Simple wooden or metal constructions suffice as long as the mirrors and their mountings are free of vibration.

Underwater periscope
A version of the periscope can be used to obtain underwater shots. This is particularly useful where models are being filmed under water, but where no camera diving-bell or observation windows exist.

Again, the periscope may be constructed of wood or metal, but all joints must be treated with a waterproofing compound. The lower mirror port must be covered with a sheet of plate glass to prevent water entering the periscope and the whole construction must be weighted to counteract the buoyancy of the internal air.

Underwater lighting
Underwater scenes must be illuminated and if a waterproof lamp is not available, the periscope described above can be used to beam light down from the floor above the studio tank to a point below the water level.

Snorkel shots
New types of lenses have been developed to capture extraordinarily close-up pictures of insects. Used to record certain special effects they can achieve results which would be unattainable from conventional optics. The eye-line of a dragonfly as it skims across the surface of a lake could be typical of the use to which these lenses are put.

But, of course, they are not simply supplementary attachments screwed to the fronts of cameras; they transmit their pictures via a series of tiny mirrors and lenses enclosed in long metal periscopes. The cameras themselves (which must be vibration-proof) are carried on large iron rigs which travel on heavy rails.

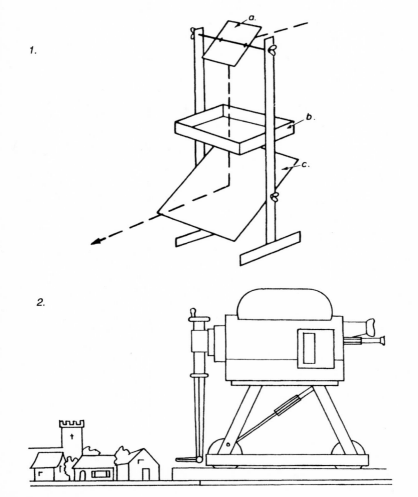

PERISCOPES

1. Periscope

A periscope device with adjustable mirrors. This may be used as a conventional periscope to get low angle shots, but when the glass-bottomed tray is brought into use it may be used for trick shots and special effects work. Water rippled in the tray gives a break-up effect. Pictures or models laid on the glass can be combined with the main picture. a, Small adjustable mirror. b, Glass-bottomed tray. c, Large adjustable mirror.

2. A periscopic camera lens

A snorkel camera with a special periscopic lens can be used to record pictures of a model from a scaled down person's eye level. This lens can also simulate pictures of such things as a dragonfly skimming over the surface of a lake.

Polystyrene Fabrication and Modelling

Expanded polystyrene is now generally accepted as being one of the most versatile materials in use in TV and movie studios. Although it has certain properties which render it liable to be classed as a fire-risk, there are grades available which are sufficiently fire retardant to pass the regulations in most studios. Its lightness and strength make it ideal for the production of large props and scenic items while the speed with which it can be worked makes it an attractive material where time and money are important.

Cutting and shaping
Large pieces of expanded polystyrene can be cut with a hand saw but where pieces need shaping it is better to use a sharp thin-bladed knife. An ideal tool is a hack-saw blade that has been ground and sharpened, but it is necessary to hone this frequently during work. A sharp knife of this kind makes it possible to carve the material into elaborate shapes and to produce sculptural items or bas-relief work.

Joining
Expanded polystyrene can be cemented, but the glue chosen must not contain those solvents that melt the material. Recommended adhesives are available from suppliers. Awkward joints can be strengthened by the insertion of sharpened wooden dowels before cementing.

Finishing
A smooth finish can be obtained by sanding, but this should not be carried out after surface treatment with paint or filler. The softer polystyrene sands faster than the surface treatment causing uneven patches to appear.

Most fillers and paints adhere firmly to expanded polystyrene, but one of the most satisfactory finishes for use where the item is likely to receive harsh treatment is latex. The aqueous variety used for casting (page 44) can be applied with a brush and if further reinforcing is required, muslin can be laid over the surface as the latex is brushed on.

Aerosol spray paints containing solvent should be avoided, but emulsion paint works well.

For the production of rocks, chunks of polystyrene can be burnt with a flame torch. The surface melts, creating a rough cratered effect closely resembling rock or stone. This treatment gives the material a hard, glazed texture, more brittle than the normal expanded polystyrene. WARNING: All such work must be done in the open air and every precaution taken against breathing the fumes.

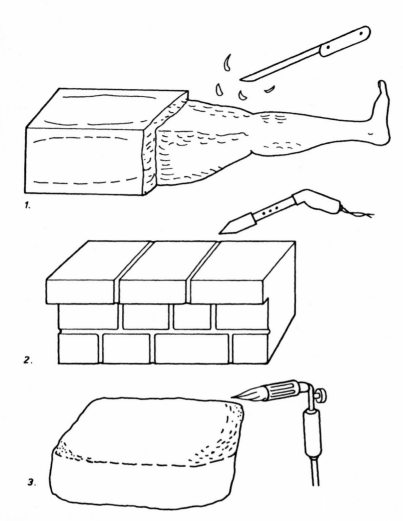

EXPANDED POLYSTYRENE

1. Shaping
Expanded polystyrene may be shaped with a sharp, thin-bladed knife that is kept constantly honed.

2. Patterns
Patterns may be engraved with a hot iron.

3. Forming
Hard stony surfaces can be imitated by melting the surface with a blowtorch. Where heat is applied to this material the fumes should not be inhaled.

33

Plastic Forming Machines

Two machines which aid the effects designer are the vacuum-forming machine and the expanded-polystyrene cutter. They are obtainable commercially, but where it would be uneconomical to buy them, they can be built cheaply and simply for short-term usage.

Expanded-polystyrene cutter

This comprises a work-top and an overhead beam which supports an electrically heated wire. Its function is to aid the cutting of small, complicated shapes in expanded-polystyrene in the same way that the fret or jigsaw cuts plywood. It also allows parallel slices or strips to be cut from block material. The work bench supports an arm to which is fastened one end of a nickel-chrome wire. The other end is fastened under the table and is spring-loaded to retain tension. The voltage is about 20-30V. The wire should reach no more than black heat as the insulation factor of the polystyrene causes a rapid temperature rise inside the material during cutting.

An adjustable guide on the bench facilitates the cutting of strips.

Vacuum-forming machine

Small items formed from lightweight, plastic sheet speed up many operations in the property-making field and the versatility of the vacuum-forming process is well appreciated in a busy effects workshop.

The device has a flat work-top under which is fitted a cylinder and a vacuum pump. The cylinder has a tap at the top which permits it, once it is partially exhausted, to suck air from the top of the bench.

The other two components are a double frame for holding the plastic sheet and an electrical heating-element.

The plastic sheet should be clamped in the frame and held down over the object to be reproduced. The heater is then lowered to a few inches from the surface and the plastic is heated until it begins to sag. At this point the heater is removed and the vacuum vessel is switched to 'suck'. The air exhausting from the lower part of the frame draws the heated plastic down onto the master object, producing a faithful reproduction.

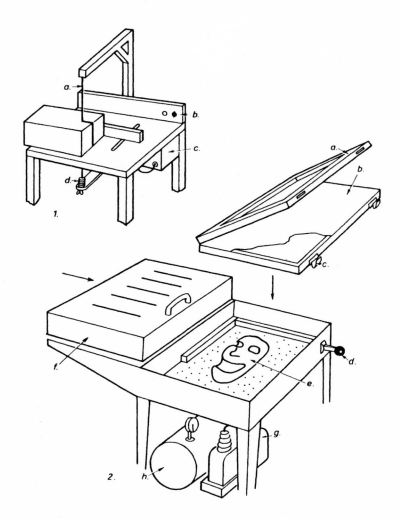

PLASTIC FORMING MACHINES

1. Hot-wire cutting
A table with a tensioned hot wire used to cut slices from blocks of expanded polystyrene. It may also be used to cut patterns in sheet material. a, Hot wire. b, Switch and indicator lamp. c, Low-voltage transformer. d, Tension spring.

2. Forming sheet plastic
Plastic sheet held in a rectangular clamp is heated until it becomes pliable. It is then drawn down by suction onto a master where it cools and forms a rigid copy of the original. a, Frame. b, Plastic sheet. c, Clamp. d, Vacuum control. e, Master. f, Movable heater. g, Vacuum pump. h, Vacuum cylinder.

35

Plaster of Paris

Plaster of Paris is used extensively in movie and TV studios. It has a variety of uses and few other materials are as versatile. It is used for the making of moulds for casting glass-fibre and resins and is also used for the making of statues, breaking crockery and scenic items.

Mixing the plaster

Plaster must always be added to water and never the other way about. Assess the quantity needed and pour that much water into a plastic bowl. Then, using a cup, add the plaster until dry material builds up above the level of the water. At this point stir thoroughly until a lump-free, smooth, creamy mixture results. Test by dipping a finger into the mix. When withdrawn, the finger should be evenly coated with a thin creamy plaster.

Well mixed plaster sets quickly, so it is important that no more than is required is mixed at a time. The residue that sets in the bowl can, when hard, be broken out by flexing the bowl.

Release agents

Plaster adheres to many things and, of course, sticks very firmly to other plaster. If it is required to take a plaster reproduction from a plaster mould a suitable release agent must be used. There are several proprietary substances available, but for general use shellac may be used to coat the mould. This should be done when the mould is absolutely dry and two or even three thin coats are usually necessary to provide a good seal.

Before use, the shellac should be given a light brush over with wax polish.

Clay also acts as a barrier to prevent plaster sticking to plaster. Thin walls or fences of clay are used to delineate the halves of a mould when it is being cast. Sometimes the clay is used in the form of strips and at other times it is applied directly to the plaster as a diluted wash. Thinned down with water and brushed on it provides an adequate parting agent.

Miscellaneous

To accelerate the setting of plaster add a little alum to the water before the mixing process.

To slow down the setting time add a small amount of size to the water. Stale beer also works well.

If plaster is worked continuously instead of allowing it to set and harden the resultant 'killed' mixture provides a good material for repairing damaged plaster work. It can be pressed into holes and cracks with a thin bladed knife and sanded when dry.

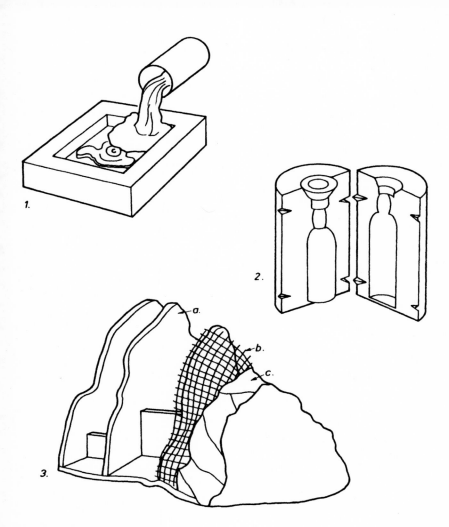

PLASTER OF PARIS

1. Open moulds
Plaster of Paris is used for casting objects in open moulds. These moulds are usually flexible to facilitate removal of the cast.

2. Plaster moulds
Plaster is also used to make moulds from which flexible articles are cast.

3. Scenic items
Plaster applied to scrim or open-weave cloth is often used in the construction of such scenic items as rocks. a, Timber. b, Wire netting. c, Cloth.

37

Plaster Turning

Freshly mixed plaster of Paris hardens within a few minutes and during that time it is possible to model it into regular shapes by pouring and turning. This is useful for producing cylindrical or spherical items without the use of a lathe.

Horizontal method
A horizontal spindle on which has been securely fastened some anchoring material (such as cloth or bandage) is laid in two vee-shaped stocks. A shaped metal profile is then fixed in a suitable position (angled so that wet plaster will run back from its edge) and the plaster is poured onto the spindle while it is slowly rotated. As the wet plaster builds up it is scraped away by the profile, producing a smooth and uniform item. This method is useful for making master items for the moulding or vacuum-forming processes.

Vertical method
Where large and heavy amounts of plaster are involved it is not so easy to use the rotating spindle method. An alternative is to perform the action vertically, with a rotating profile working around a static amount of plaster.

A vertically-mounted tube fitted firmly to a baseboard acts as a centre point. In this is placed a rod, to the top end of which is attached the profile. The plaster is poured onto the baseboard while the profile is slowly rotated, forming the obiect from the bottom upward.

In both these methods fluid plaster cleared away by the profile can be scooped up and re-poured over the article. Where very large amounts of plaster are being used it is necessary to stop the operation from time to time and mix fresh plaster. At this stage all dried swarf should be cleared away.

When large articles are being made the centre mass can be built up with pieces of expanded polystyrene or other coarse filler material, using the plaster only for the outer layer. With the vertical method female shapes can be turned if a strong supporting outer wall is made to acccommodate the plaster. Turning must be done carefully because the fluid material runs to the bottom and has to be scooped out as the work progresses.

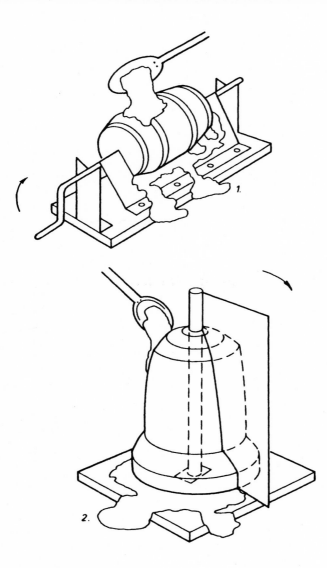

PLASTER TURNING

1. Revolving spindle
A method of using liquid plaster to create a barrel shaped object. The object is revolved against a stationary profile.

2. Revolving profile
To form a large plaster bell, the profile is revolved while the object is held stationary.

Mould Making

Plaster moulds used for the reproduction of items in resin, wax or latex are either open moulds for straightforward pouring or enclosed (piece) moulds comprising two or more interlocking pieces used for swilling or casting.

Flexible moulds, usually backed with plaster supporting-cradles and known as 'case' moulds are used for laying up glass-fibre objects or for casting complicated items where there are problems connected with undercuts or detail that could not be withdrawn from an inflexible plaster mould.

How to make a two-piece mould

Place the master to be moulded on a flat board and surround half of it with clay. Finish the edge of the clay cleanly and uniformly around the master to provide a firm support for the top half of the mould.

Using a cup, pour the freshly mixed plaster over the item until a thin coat has completely covered the surface. Repeat this action several times until a thick and uniform coat has been built up over the master.

Endeavour to flatten the top of the mould with a tool as the pouring progresses, so that it can stand steadily when you turn it over for the next operation. Allow plaster to harden and clean tools and utensils.

Invert the mould and remove all the clay. *Do not* disturb the master embedded in the first half of the mould.

Using a sharp knife, cut three tapering 'vee' slots in the edge of the mould. These will act as registers when the two halves come together for moulding.

Using a diluted clay wash, paint the edge where the second half will meet the first.

Repeat the first pouring operation until the second half has built up.

Allow plenty of time for plaster to harden then separate the mould and remove the master item.

Cut a pouring hole in the edge of one of the halves where it will not mar the reproduction.

Keep the halves of the mould together with adhesive tape or string and write on the outside what it is.

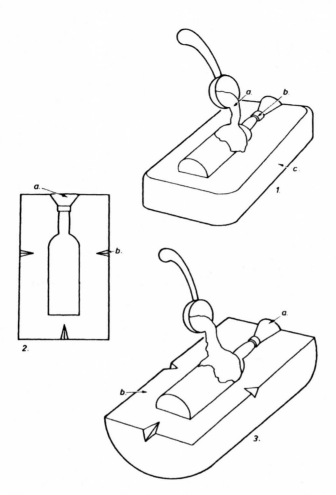

MOULD MAKING

1. First half-mould
The master is embedded in a block of clay and plaster is poured over it to form one half of the mould. a, Plaster. b, Master. c, Clay.

2. Preparing the mould
The poured half of the plaster mould. The clay has been removed and the master now lies embedded in plaster. Location notches are cut, and a clay plug formed for the pouring hole. a, Clay plug. b, Location notches.

3. Second half-mould
Plaster is poured on to a clay wash on the first half and flows into the locator notches to form an interlocking second mould. a, Clay plug. b, Clay wash.

Flexible Moulds

Although fibreglass mouldings and plaster casts can be produced from plaster piece-moulds, it is more convenient to cast them in moulds that are flexible. These need fewer sections and allow the casting to be withdrawn without danger of breakage or the trapping of undercuts. Because they *are* flexible each section must be encased in a thick layer of plaster, which will act as a support. Thereafter the two elements should never be separated.

Most articles will remove cleanly from a two-piece mould, but complicated shapes may demand more.

Hot melt

A proprietary material (Vinamold) which requires to be melted in special temperature-controlled heating equipment is poured over an object and allowed to cool. If the object is made of plaster it must be thoroughly dried and coated with a sealant.

Vinamold retains its shape and flexibility for a very long time and can be used to cast dozens of objects without loss of detail. After use it can be re-melted.

Small amounts of Vinamold may be *very* slowly heated in a saucepan, but the operation must be closely monitored.

Silicone rubber

This material, which cannot be reused, consists of a two-part mix in which a catalyst is added to the body material prior to pouring. Slowly the catalyst works and the liquid turns to a rubber-like substance. It retains its shape and detail and can be stored for long periods.

When poured (as with similar moulding materials) it should not be allowed to flow over the master, but should be introduced in such a fashion that it rises upwards, enveloping the master from below. This ensures that the material will enter undercuts without trapping air. Deep undercuts may require the master and its case to be tilted.

Silicone rubber sections must be encased in plaster.

Latex

The tough white latex (page 44) used for the production of flexible props may be employed for the making of moulds, but is less versatile than silicone rubber.

Registration

The plaster cases which stabilise flexible moulds should have 'vees' and 'notches' along their edges to provide a register.

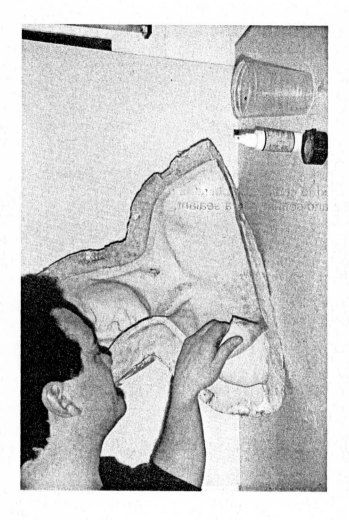

FLEXIBLE MOULDS

Flexible rubber or other materials used for casting must be supported by plaster case moulds. Although a corner is shown being lifted here, it is unwise ever to fully separate the two.

Latex Casting

One of the most versatile materials, aqueous-based liquid latex may be poured into moulds to reproduce all sorts of property items and costume embellishments. It is available in both heavy and light grades.

Casting latex
Poured into plaster moulds, latex adheres to the walls, whereupon the water content soaks into the plaster leaving the latex behind.

Moulds should have their internal surfaces clean, dry and uncontaminated with release agents. Latex is poured in through a convenient hole and after being swilled around is emptied out. This action should be repeated at least three times at intervals of 30 minutes allowing each application to thoroughly coat the internal surface of the mould.

The cast may be left to dry naturally, but it is more convenient to put it in a moderate oven. The heat cures the latex and dries out the mould.

Grade
The heavy grade of castng latex may be used for making many items ranging from mock armour to sticks and iron bars used in fight scenes. Latex items have the advantage that they can take a great deal of punishment without suffering damage.

The lighter grade may be used in the construction of face-masks to be worn by actors. With eye and mouth holes cut out, the latex mask can, by the application of make-up, be made to blend into the natural face to a degree where it is almost impossible to tell where the joins occur.

Another use for the lighter grade is in the making of insects, animals and medical specimens.

Vegetables, meats and fish can also be cast easily and cheaply.

Finish
Latex can be coloured with most paints and enamels and even with varnishes and lacquers.These finishes crack if severely handled, but seldom flake off.

Other uses
Applied with a brush, latex painted over expanded polystyrene gives it a hard resilient coating that is useful for artificial bricks and rocks.

Bandage wound round an actor's leg and coated with latex can be cut off when dry and used later as a simulated plaster cast

A puddle of latex poured onto a sheet of glass and allowed to dry may be painted to resemble oil, paint, molasses, etc. Laid on the floor in the studio it looks real without being messy. Useful for applying to cookers, expensive rented furniture, carpets, etc.

Latex is poured into a dry plaster piece mould.

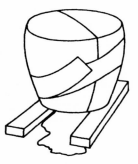

After being allowed to stand for a while the mould is inverted and drained.

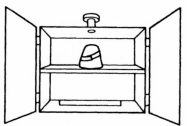

The mould is left in an oven to cure.

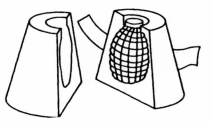

The mould is opened and the cast removed.

Glass Fibre Lay-Ups and Casting Resin

Cold-setting polyester resins usually consist of the resin, a hardener and a catalyst. When mixed, they set as a hard brittle compound. In itself the resin is not structurally tough but when combined with strands of glass fibre it produces a material which is well known for lightness and strength.

Lay-up
The best moulds for resin and glass fibre are made from latex or flexible moulding compound supported by a thick plaster backing to prevent them distorting. If a plaster-of-Paris mould is used it must be treated with a suitable release agent.

First, a layer of resin known as the gel coat is applied to the surface of the mould with a brush. It is allowed to harden slightly so that the glass fibre, which is applied next, does not penetrate and spoil the surface.

The glass is obtainable either as a woven material or in chopped strands. It is laid, a piece at a time, on the gel coat, and impregnated with a second application of resin, firmly brushed into the glass. The layering process may be repeated as many times as necessary to build up the required thickness.

The gel coat may contain a pigment to give the finished article a colour.

Casting
Resin can be poured into moulds to produce cast objects. Powdered metals added to the first coat in the mould (it is wasteful to use them for the entire pour) can make the cast resin look remarkably like metal. This is useful when prop knives and weapons are being made. It is also a cheap and easy method of simulating bronze busts, brass medallions and aluminium fittings.

Finishing
The finished cast must be lightly sanded with an abrasive material. Usually 'wet and dry' paper works well. The cast should then be buffed up with a rag and metal polish as would be the case with real metal.

To improve the look of certain 'metal' casts it is possible to wipe on colours and treatments. If the article purports to be bronze, green paint may be applied to the surface and then wiped clean. The residue left behind in the low lying areas gives a satisfactory patina of age. Brown ochre for brass and graphite for steel and aluminium give equally satisfactory results. If an article is to look rusty, it should be varnished, partially wiped clean and then dusted with cocoa.

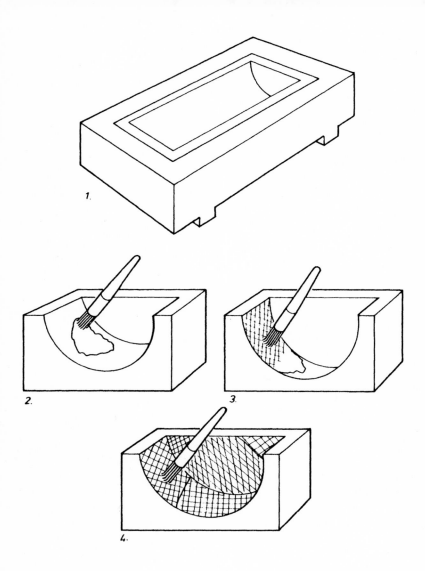

GLASS FIBRE LAY-UP

1. Case moulds – flexible moulds supported by plaster cases – are often used for glass fibre lay-ups.
2. Resin is applied to the internal surfaces of the mould and allowed to gel.
3. Glass fibre is brushed firmly onto the resin and more resin is brushed into the weave of the material.
4. Overlapping pieces are applied until the mould is covered.

47

Matte and Glass Shots

There are many ways of increasing the area of a scene without building scenery or adding to the amount of floor space. The techniques used not only give additional dimensions, but also permit effects to be obtained that might be impossible in real terms.

Matte shots

These are usually associated with film, the TV equivalent being the electronic inlay and overlay devices for obtaining similar results.

Briefly, a film matte is the process by which part of a frame is left unexposed so that it can later be used to record another picture. In this way two components may be used to produce a single picture on one negative. The simplest example is where a black card is positioned in front of the camera so that only half a picture is recorded. The film is then rewound without moving the position of the camera and the black card is repositioned to obscure the part of the scene that has already been filmed. The composite picture is called a split screen. It permits an actor to appear as two people in the same shot. Matte work is the province of the cameraman and the processing laboratories and involves some very complicated processes. The most versatile is known as travelling matte where backgrounds can be inserted behind actors who have previously played their scene against a coloured backing.

Glass shots

Glass shots are often used where it is required to show a ceiling without actually constructing one. The technique is to set a sheet of glass in front of the camera and for the false ceiling to be painted directly on the glass. This must be done with constant reference to the camera eyepiece to ensure that the painting lines up with the studio set. The size of the painting and its distance from the camera are governed by the fact that both scene and foreground glass must be in focus.

As the sheet of glass reflects anything in front of it, the camera must be in a darkened area or surrounded by black drapes.

Glass is used when particularly fine work or disconnected items have to appear in the scene, but there are many instances when it can be dispensed with and a simple cardboard cut-out employed. This is possible when skies, landscapes or seascapes are included in a scene.

The card, painted to blend with the scenery, can be made to match at some convenient natural boundary – such as the horizon or the ridge of a roof. For a false ceiling for studio scenes the tops of flats on the set and the bottom of a piece of card blend quite satisfactorily.

The glass shot does not always require the work of an artist: cut-out photographs, provided they are big enough, can be used to supplement the scene.

48

MATTE AND GLASS SHOTS

1. Painted scenery
By using pictures painted on glass much time and money can be saved in construction of scenery. The example shown here demonstrates how the top half of an oil rig is aligned with a scenic base built on location. Reflections in the glass can be troublesome and black boards – or even complete black cabins – must be erected to shield the glass. a, Black sheet. b, Painted glass. c, Scenic base. d, Final picture.

2. Ceilings
The painted glass technique is often used to provide ceilings for interior sets in the studio.

49

Models and Miniatures

Another method of counterfeiting a scene is to use a model – a technique as old as movie-making itself.

Employed in this fashion the model is called a miniature. When designed to be only part of a scene it is referred to as a hanging miniature.

In its most elementary form a miniature could be a model landscape, a building or even a single window in the wall of a house.

The advantage of employing a miniature is that it can be more economic than building scenery or finding a suitable location. Furthermore an exterior model erected and recorded indoors will be unaffected by weather.

Static shots

An ancillary set in the studio of, say, the end wall of a ballroom would be transformed if it were to be augmented with two side walls. Scale models of these positioned in front of the set would give the effect of a three-sided room. Even if the sequence were to involve nothing more than a servant entering and lighting some candles, the small amount of model-making effort would give the set a breadth and depth out of all proportion to the space it occupied in the studio.

Another example might feature the hold of a cargo ship in which someone had to examine its contents. To fill a TV studio with dozens of packing cases would be impractical, and so a sequence employing a hanging miniature in front of the camera and a few life-sized crates on the floor could be devised.

Where sequences call for inter-cutting between the set and the miniature it is important to ensure that the models do not attempt to replicate their full-sized counterparts – the differences in texture and finish will be quite apparent. In this case, the hold of a ship, presumably containing many different objects, would enable any disparity to be disguised.

Shots with action

The above examples illustrate the use of static models, but miniatures are often designed to include some form of animation. A flashing lighthouse or a distant building in which a window lights up are among the simplest. But where more complicated scenes include working parts or moving machinery it could be less costly to build a model than to construct a full sized set.

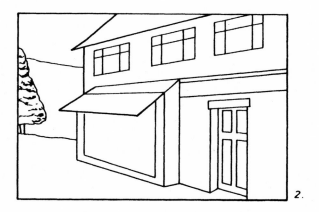

1.

2.

MODEL SHOTS

1. Models to set the scene
Three dimensional models are often used to establish a scene, and in some cases they may have to be very detailed.

2. Part-model construction
It is sometimes simpler to use a photograph with only part of the model built in three dimensions. This is particularly useful if some action has to take place on what would otherwise be a complicated model.

51

Action Miniatures

Because the purpose of a miniature is to convince viewers that they are looking at a real-life scene, movements on an action miniature must be correctly scaled. This implies that distances and times must be co-related and that every motion is recorded at the right speed.

Water
Model ship sequences in movies are among the finest special effects created for the medium, but they are invariably filmed on huge outdoor tanks. (The one at Pinewood Studios is 230ft (70.1m) wide backed by a 60ft (18.3m) high false sky.) Nevertheless quite creditable results can be obtained on smaller tanks constructed from tarpaulins.

Storm sequences require the use of wind machines, wave paddles and foam mixtures, but the drops of water that are thrown up have a natural, unalterable size, which can mar the illusion. Water-softening chemicals (not detergent, which produces troublesome surface bubbles) may be used to lessen the viscosity and prevent drops clinging to the sides of models.

Fire
Flames do not scale down satisfactorily and should never be used on very small models. Slow motion in these circumstances is essential but even with this assistance flames which are too small take on an oily, unnatural quality.

Trains
Model trains rock from side to side on their tiny tracks, but slowed down by high-speed recording, this movement can look remarkably realistic.

Explosions and demolition
Providing they are built as big as possible and are supplied with plenty of scale debris and dust at the source of the explosion, model buildings which have to be blown up generally perform well. It is usual to make them in sections which are merely laid or stood in position.

Tall buildings and skyscrapers need special attention at ground level, where in real life the concrete rubble would fall. One trick is to place cement dust at the foot of the model and blow it outwards with compressed air. This adds drama and obscures the lower half of the building.

Hanging Miniatures

A miniature is a model buit to look like a full-sized scene, whereas a hanging miniature is used to *supplement* a scene. Placed between the camera and the set it should blend in in such a way that the difference in scale is undetectable. In its simplest form it could be, say, a mountain range to fill the upper half of a studio scene. Elaborate roofs and ceilings may be added at a fraction of the cost of building their full-sized counterparts, while such scenic requirements as a ship's boiler room or an underground cave could be simulated using only a few items of full-sized scenery. The time and effort saved in turning round a studio can be appreciated.

As with glass mattes, the models can be recorded separately and added to the tape or film as a post-production process, but the advantage of employing a hanging miniature *during* the actual recording is that the components can be aligned in the camera viewfinder or by looking at the studio monitor.

Chroma key
In the case of television, rather than placing the model in front of the main camera, it is usual to record it on a second camera. With a blue screen behind the main set the model can be overlaid by the use of chroma key (page 66). In this way both the model and the set can be correctly aligned, individually lit and independently focused.

Outdoors
If a miniature is used outdoors, both it and the location will be lit from the same source (the sun and the sky) and to the same intensity. This ensures that, whatever the conditions, the shadows on both will match – something that could not be guaranteed with a painted matte.

Fixing
Fixing a hanging miniature in the studio is a relatively simple matter. Sometimes, as its name suggests, it is simply hung. Outdoors, however, wind can play havoc with flimsy models. When small or fine unsupported details must be included they can be stuck to a sheet of glass incorporated in the model.

Hanging Miniatures - Applications 1

Hanging miniatures may be used for so many purposes it would be pointless to consider a list of examples. Nevertheless as certain conventions apply a few are given here.

Background
One of the most frequently called-for additions to a scene is, of course, the sky – with the possible inclusion of sea or land.

In the movie studio it is simply a matter of blanking out the existing background and adding a painting or sky-plate. However, when some sort of animation is required a hanging miniature must be created – for an erupting volcano or a distant camp-fire, for instance.

Economics
Hanging miniatures are used to save time and money – a typical example being a situation in which someone is standing, say, outside a prison. Posing an actor against a suitable wall and positioning a model of a prison in front of the camera would suffice for a short sequence or a comedy sketch. The reason for using a model instead of a painting is that it gives a (limited) choice of camera positions.

Realisation
Miniatures are also created because the required location or item does not exist. Visualise a huge sci-fi spacecraft, supported on extending legs with a ladder leading up to an illuminated entry port. There being little chance of hiring such a giant prop, the hanging miniature would provide the answer. The entire thing could be constructed as a model with only the ladder being a full-sized component. If a person had to ascend or descend this ladder a light shone from above would appear to be coming from the open port of the spaceship.

Movement
Provided the optics of a camera are in line and that the film or TV receptor plate is on, or close to, the pivoting point of the camera, it is possible to zoom, pan and tilt on the miniature without the deception becoming apparent. However, some modern optical arrangements do produce a picture shift. (Don't rely on a camcorder to replicate the optics of a studio camera.) It is not feasible to track or crab the camera dolly.

54

MINIATURES

1. Hanging miniatures
Models suspended or supported in front of the camera can be made to seem part of the scene.

2. Advantages
Miniatures often give better results than glass shots. The light that falls on the main scene also illuminates the model, giving similar conditions of contrast and shadows. This technique gives greater choice of camera angles.

55

Hanging Miniatures – Applications 2

Some directors have a reluctance to use hanging miniatures because the choice of shots moves out of their control. Nevertheless there are times when even the most unwilling director must accept that a technique of this kind is the only method of obtaining something difficult or dangerous.

The safety bonus
Visualise a scene in which a light aircraft has to fly into the open doors of a factory. A stunt flyer might be willing to undertake the job, but the insurance premiums would be prohibitive. The hanging model, however, would provide a classic solution.

For this sequence it would be necessary to find a suitable building (many exist on private airfields) which would then be extended by the use of a model. From the camera position this would have to appear as one complete edifice with large open doors in the appropriate position. The aircraft would need only to fly *past* the original building to make it appear that it had actually flown inside.

Consider another dramatic scene in which a speedboat careers into a lake-side boat-house, which then explodes in a huge fireball. The hanging miniature would once again prove to be a 'life-saver'.

Reflections in the water
Used with water scenes a hanging miniature can be very effective, but there are certain limiting factors. Water moves and this can expose the matte line between itself and the model. It also reflects.

Reflections in moving water are so broken that they give little trouble. However, on still water they can cause problems particularly if the background on the model is very different from the one it is shielding. The reflection of a house on the opposite bank would show, if only by areas of colour, a marked contrast with a model of, say, the Amazonian jungle or an icy glacier.

1.

2.

3.

HANGING MINIATURES – APPLICATION 2

Test photograph taken at a garden centre in which it was necessary to hide an untidy background.
1. The ground as it was.
2. A preliminary miniature clamped to supports.
3. The test results showing a merge between the background and the painted miniature.

Model Landscapes

Model landscapes for TV purposes are usually built on a firm base-board with a hardboard backing on which the sky is painted. For movie productions (where the definition must be greater) miniature land-scapes are often far from 'miniature', occasionally filling entire studios.

Constructed of materials such as wood, card, plaster, expanded polystyrene and so on, landscapes seldom need to be built with any degree of permanence. Sand heaped on to the base-board and sprinkled with coloured sawdust will resemble rolling hills and is easier to modify than a solid construction of plaster or sculptured polystyrene.

Fields and trees

For conventional terrestrial scenes, trees, bushes and other forms of vegetation can be created from a variety of natural and man-made materials. Most popular is lichen moss, which can be dyed and used to simulate small bushes and hedges. Fastened to wire stalks it can look like miniature deciduous trees.

Conifers can be reproduced by cutting and shaping laboratory bottle brushes and, after a spray of adhesive, dipping them in dyed sawdust.

Small pieces of torn sponge or plastic foam can be painted to resemble vegetation, but some of the most convincing mini-plants and bushes can be obtained from dried weeds and wild flowers.

Dyed sawdust is used for ground treatments where it resembles ploughed earth or verdant fields. A variety of greens, ochres, yellows, browns and black should be used and the different colours scattered one upon another in variations.

Perspective

To resemble its full-size counterpart a landscape model should be built with a certain amount of false perspective. Roads should be wide near the lens and narrow towards the horizon. Fields should be compressed as they recede.

Matte lines

The division between a miniature and the real scene is, of course, in full view. It is therefore necessary to create a join in which it passes unnoticed. A sharp line such as the top of a wall or the side of a building can provide a good merging point, but where gardens or rugged landscapes are involved it is possible to camouflage the join by affixing small pieces of lichen moss or other materials to the front of the miniature's base-board.

MODEL LANDSCAPES

Model trees can be made by twisting brush hairs in a loop of wire. This is best done with a hand-drill and a fixed anchor point such as a nail.

The simplest shape to make is the conifer, but many other varieties can be obtained by cutting and shaping the hairs with nail scissors.

Sprayed with glue and dipped in coloured sawdust, these tiny trees can look extremely lifelike

Model Ships

Commensurate with the size of the tank or the area of water available, model ships should be as large as possible. It is often easier to handle and film a big model than a small one. Large ships have a better relationship with the wave scale and manoeuvre better on water. Another bonus is that it is generally easier to construct the detail on large models and, although the cost of materials is likely to be higher, the speed of work is often quicker.

Sub-frame
Waves generated on the studio tank can cause the model ship to bob up and down in an uncharacteristic fashion. To eliminate this it is possible to construct a sub-frame to which the hull can be attached by rods. The frame can be manipulated from below, imparting a lifelike roll-and-pitch movement to the model above.

Anchored in this fasion the model cannot of course travel forward, but if water is made to flow past the hull, the effect is the same as forward motion of the boat.

Wakes and bow waves
To improve the illusion of forward motion it is usual to provide the model with a false wake and false bow-waves. White liquid stored in tanks in the hull or fed by submerged pipes can be made to flow from waterline holes at the stern of the ship, the resultant trail appearing most effective. Similarly, small waves on either side of the bows can be contrived by fixing small backward facing tubes just below the water. These effects look best when the ship is actually being propelled (or pulled by an underwater line) on a large tank or on open water.

Outdoors
Ships on outdoor lakes or rivers or even the sea can be driven by battery-powered screws. It is seldom practical to have these connected to underwater power lines, so radio control should be employed to switch the motor and to control the rudder. It is often found that extended keels help to damp down unwanted rolling movements.

Submarine shots
'Underwater' shots of submarines can be filmed in the dry if the models are hung on wires in front of a green background. Careful lighting can create the illusion that the vessel is actually under water, particularly if a water ripple effect is projected on the upper part of the backing and onto the submarine itself.

Another method is to use the model against front or rear scenic projection of an underwater setting.

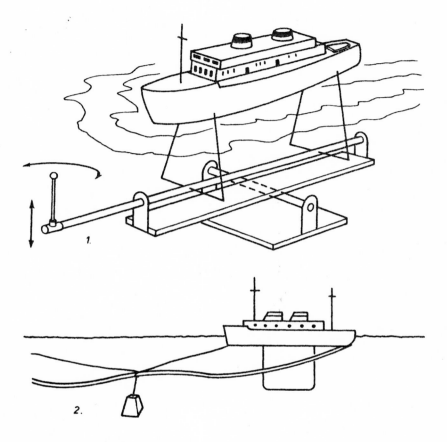

MODEL SHIPS

1. Storm sequences
Model ships appearing in storm sequences are best anchored to a fixed base which
can be manipulated to impart a realistic pitch and roll action.

2. Towing precautions
Models being towed should have their tow lines weighted to keep them below water
level. Extended keels reduce unnatural motion caused by the towing action. Take care
that the wake from the towing vessel does not appear in the shot

61

Model Seas

The filming of model ships in studio or improvised tanks should not be undertaken lightly as these scenes are among the most difficult to create with satisfactory realism. Clever editing and subliminal views do much to make the best of unconvincing material, but there is no doubt that a bad model shot can destroy a dramatic situation rather than support it.

Miniature sea

A seascape comprising a placid lagoon or the view of a distant desert island is not too difficult to create. This type of miniature can be set up in a shallow plastic-lined tank erected at camera lens height and filmed in a studio. Where the script calls for complicated action, however, such as a ship foundering in a storm or a submarine surfacing, the model must be operated in a robustly constructed tank situated on the floor or in a proper studio tank.

In all cases where the scene is supposed to take place in daylight, the tank must be backed by a light sky cloth or a back projection screen. Without such an area of flat light to reflect on the surface of the water, the scene looks like a night shot.

Waves

Waves can be produced simply by paddling flat boards fixed to the ends of poles. These should be manipulated on opposite sides of the tank, the cross-modulation producing credible miniature waves, but filming has to be at high speed to slow the waves down.

Horizon

In model tanks the waves must not disturb the horizon, which should of course appear as a straight line. One way of overcoming this problem is to have a sloping board at the back of the tank on which the waves spend themselves. To hide the board the tank must be kept filled with water, the overflow taking place at the back of the tank over the sloping board.

Model boats can be filmed on outdoor ponds and lakes, but in these cases, if the viewpoint is a low one, the horizon presents even more trouble. A solution may sometimes be found in putting down a layer of smoke over the water in the background. The smoke blends with the sky and gives the impression that the horizon is much lower than it really is.

1.

Photo: Effects Associates, Pinewood Studios

MODEL SEAS

1. Studio tank
Model ships being tested on the outdoor tank at Pinewood Studios, England. Their sizes can be gauged from the men working on them. The sky is painted on a huge cyclorama permanently erected at the back of the tank.

2. Hiding the background
Troublesome backgrounds can sometimes be eliminated if it is possible to lay down smoke. Blending with both water and sky this falsifies the horizon level giving the model ship a more realistic scale.

63

Scenic Projection

This is the system where large photographic backgrounds are projected on a screen behind the action. It is cheap, easy to use and enables very realistic indoor or outdoor scenes to be re-created in the studio.

It can be employed in both movie and TV studios and can provide moving as well as static backgrounds.

When moving subjects are required, the recording camera and the projector must be interlocked to ensure that the shutter of the camera is synchronised with the shutter of the projector.

Back projection

This is the oldest and most widely used form of projection, but demands more studio space than other systems. The projector is situated behind a transluscent screen which itself is placed behind the studio scene. A very powerful projector is required because the screen absorbs a great deal of the illumination. To obtain maximum benefit from the available light the camera should be positioned on the same axis as the projector.

Smaller set-ups are used to obtain the moving scenes in the rear windows of cars in the studio.

Front-axial projection

This is more economical in the use of space as the projector is positioned in front of the screen which can therefore be placed at the rear of the studio.

The screen, consisting of a flexible material covered with millions of tiny glass beads has the unique property of being able to reflect the light that strikes it back along the path from which it came.

This of course implies that all the light is reflected back to the projector. To make the system work it is necessary to install a beam-splitter between the projector and the recording camera so that some of the light returning from the screen is diverted to the camera. The screen material reflects so efficiently that a domestic 35mm slide projector can be used to provide large background scenes, while light reflected from actors in the projector beam is insufficient to affect the film.

Application

Front-axial screen material can be cut up and used to provide multi-plane layouts. For instance a projected picture of a house against sky could be split into two parts, the house being beamed on to a profiled cut-out and the sky on to the studio backing. A person walking from behind the cut-out would appear to come from behind the house. Useful for Lilliputian scenes where small people walk around large objects.

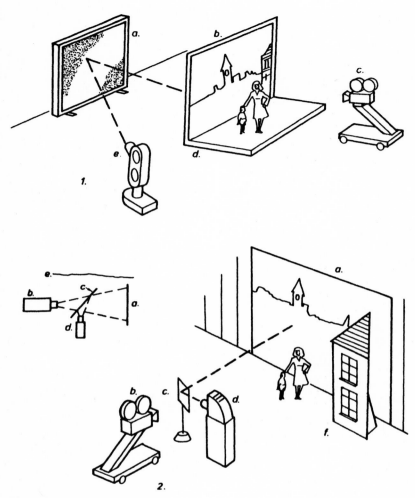

SCENIC PROJECTION

1. Back projection
Easy to set up and use, back projection requires a lot of studio space. Large mirrors are used to reduce the distance from projector to screen.
a, Mirror. b, Translucent screen. c, Camera. d, Stage. e, Movie projector.

2. Front-axial projection
More care is needed in setting up, but front axial projection uses no extra studio space and provides brighter pictures. It also permits the background picture to be split up into layers if profiled pieces of reflex screen material are positioned in front of the action. a, Reflex screen. b, Camera. c, Semi-transparent mirror. d, Projector. e, Black backing. f, Free standing profiled screen faced with reflex material.

65

Chroma Key: Colour Separation Overlay

These are the names given to an electronic method of combining the outputs from two or more TV cameras or other sources (such as film scanners, etc.). The system allows parts of one picture to be inlaid into another in such a way that the divisions cannot be detected.

The brain of the device is an electronic switch that 'flips' over when fed with a certain colour signal from the primary picture. If for instance the control colour is blue, wherever that blue appears in the original scene the switch automatically removes it and substitutes pictures from the second source.

The equipment is highly selective so that only the precise colour hue will trigger the switch, all other tones of the same colour leaving it unaffected.

What it can do
One of its chief assets is that it enables backgrounds to be inserted behind actors without the necessity for a scenic projection system. The actors perform in front of a blue backing and the background scene is supplied either from a transparency scanner or from film on a telecine machine. Alternatively, a second TV camera can be framed up on a picture or photograph in the studio.

Actors dressed in blue performing against a blue backing are invisible. This is useful for those effects where disembodied heads float around or where a person, clothed fully in blue, can manipulate props without being seen. Similarly a flying-carpet can be supported on a framework painted blue and appear to float in the sky.

The chroma key/CSO equipment is often used for caption effects. Letters on coloured backgrounds can be combined with moving film or studio shots to give any variety of effects.

Free-standing cut-outs painted blue can be used to divide the inserted material into layers. This permits actors to work around various components of the inlaid scene. For example, the crates and boxes in a warehouse scene might be no more than sections of profiled plywood coloured blue.

Limitations
Actors placed in front of blue-painted backings are bound to be illuminated from behind with that colour. This leads to coloured fringing which shows against the inserted background. Yellow is sometimes less disturbing than blue for that reason.

Any shiny surface will reflect the colour of the backing, causing break-up of the signal in that area.

Inserted backgrounds remain constant so any movement of the camera taking the primary scene cannot be tolerated.

66

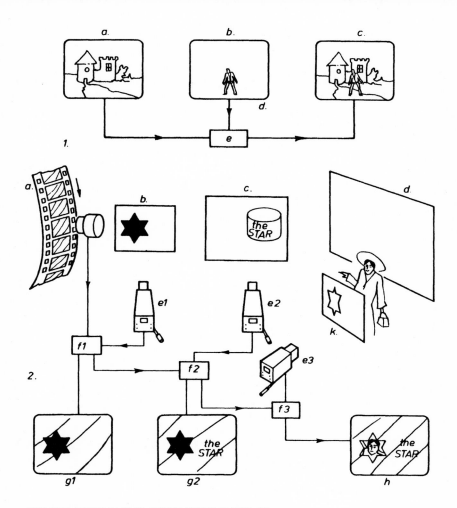

CHROMA KEY/COLOUR SEPARATION OVERLAY

1. Switching colour
The control colour switches the output from one camera to another.
a, Output from camera 1. b, Output from camera 2. c, Transmitted picture. d, Switching colour. e, Switching unit.

2. Chroma key operation
A number of sources can be combined in one final picture. This is useful for caption effects, but also has application in scenic effects.
1, Telecine film scanner. b, Caption. c, Moving caption in front of backing. d, Performer in front of backing. e, TV camera. f, Switch units. g, Outputs. h, Transmitted picture. k, Cut-out.

67

Optical Printing

Many effects can be achieved on film that are not yet possible on video tape. Carried out by specialists in the processing laboratories, optical printing offers a means of combining and integrating filmed sequences in any fashion required.

Very basically, it is a system where the original film is run through a projector and re-photographed by a movie camera. The facilities for inserting masks, altering the frame size, changing the colour, etc. are almost unlimited. It is, however, essential to consult with the lab technician before shooting as he can only use the material with which he is supplied.

Optical mattes
An obscuring mask positioned in the printer as the fresh stock is run through allows an area to remain unexposed. Different treatment can then be given to this area in a second run through the camera with an opposite mask. An example could be a scene in which a person looking at a mirror sees something other than his own reflection.

Selected frames
The optical printer can freeze action by reproducing one frame continuously. It can also run film backwards to reverse the action.

It can slow the action down by stretch printing, such as by printing every other frame twice, making two frames into three. This is useful if the original material is shot at 16 or 18 frames per second and seems a bit jerky.

'Smoothing-out' can be achieved by lightly over-printing on the middle frame, the frame before and the frame after. These additional ghost images can sometimes eradicate the jerkiness of a bad shot where something has passed too quickly across the frame.

By selecting particular frames and sequences, animation of the original film can be carried out in time to music or speech. For example, trees and flowers blowing in the wind can be made to perform to an orchestral score or animals can have their mouth movements synchronised with words.

Comic animation
For some comic sequences it is not merely sufficient to alter the speed of the action. Where the movement is to appear unreal the optical printer can be programmed to select say, every fourth frame and print it four times, imparting a jerky mechanical movement to otherwise smooth action.

68

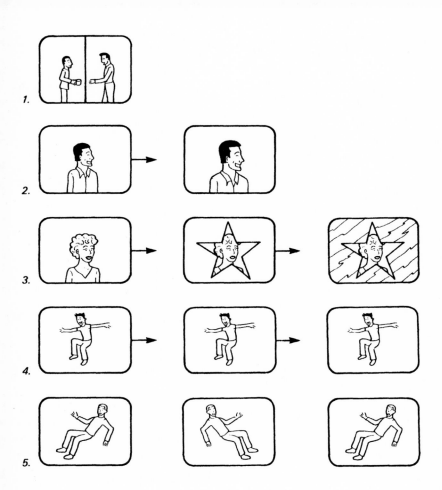

OPTICAL PRINTING

Many special effects can be achieved on film by the use of an optical printer which can modify both the subject material and the action. 1, Split screen effects. 2, Frame content can be enlarged. 3, Frame can have mask added and second background. 4, Frame can have action frozen. 5, Frames can be printed to give specific animation.

69

Underwater Sequences

Above or below the surface water is an uncooperative medium. Boats float off-station, lines and gear become entangled and props need to be heavily weighted. Nothing is easy to manoeuvre under water. Allow days, not hours, when estimating schedules.

Contamination
As many coastal seas in the Western hemisphere are too murky to permit underwater filming, sub-aqua sequences are invariably recorded in studio tanks or swimming pools. In studio tanks the water must be treated with chemicals to prevent the formation of green algae which grows rapidly in warm water under artificial lighting.

Foreshortening
Water has different optical properties from air, and the pool or tank which would seem adequately proportioned on the surface will appear narrowed and foreshortened below. The rear wall comes forward, the floor tilts up and the sides converge.

Natural growth
Tiled or concrete walls can be disguised by covering them with artificial growth. This is best done by attaching real weed, torn plastic, shredded sacking or painted cloth to garden netting.

Pre-washing
Items of scenery which have been prepared above water will carry a certain amount of dirt and dust. Everything to be submersed should first be thoroughly hosed down on clean concrete or a tarpaulin. Failure to do this could postpone filming for many hours while the water clears.

The sea bed
Sacking or hessian painted and treated with blobs of plaster can be used to cover the bottom of a tank. Loose material such as sand should never be used where it would clog the filtration plant.

False floors of this kind can be weighted down with clean rocks or stones.

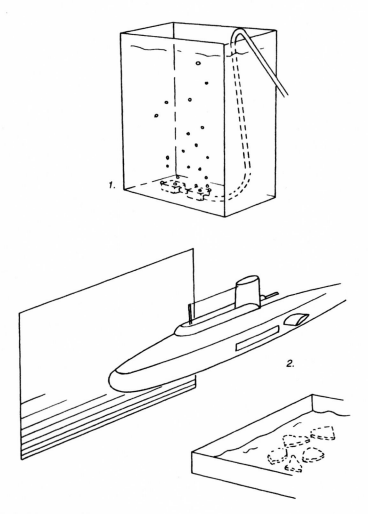

UNDERWATER SEQUENCES

1. A glass-sided bubble tank
Bubble-tanks are placed in front of screens to imply that the action is taking place underwater. Air pressure applied to fish-tank aerator blocks will produce miniature bubbles.

2. A dry submarine
Shot against a backing which is light at the top and dark at the bottom a model submarine will appear to be underwater. Rippling light on the under-side is created by shining a lamp onto pieces of broken mirror placed in a shallow tray of water. To obtain the effect the surface of the water must be gently agitated.

Water in the Studio

Effects requiring the use of water in the studio range from 'leaking taps' to epic scenes involving thousands of gallons of water. Rarely are large effects recorded in TV studios, it being more usual to pre-film them on movie stages equipped with tanks. Nevertheless, quite large areas of TV studio floors are occasionally dressed with shallow tanks representing lakes or rivers.

The simplest method of containing water on the studio floor is to lay down scene cloth or hessian (burlap) on which is placed a seamless sheet of heavy-gauge plastic, supported at its perimeter by planks.

Dump tanks
Where large amounts of water are required to surge into shot, dump tanks may be constructed from plastic lined timber. It is sensible to design tipping-tanks so that the water is always in equilibrium, to ensure that the operators have control over the rate of flow.

For water effects where the entire volume is required to be released instantly, it is possible to construct a tank where one side may be dropped by knocking out the supports.

Supplies
Where possible, piped services should be avoided in the studio. It is often a simple matter, if the effect is a small one, to use a locally situated container. This has the advantage that in the event of a mishap, the studio floor is not flooded nor the electrics sprayed with high pressure water.

One method of supplying water is to have the effect connected to a tank which can be raised or lowered. The higher the tank is raised above the outlet the greater the pressure.

The raising and lowering can be used to control certain types of effect. Typical examples are the wash-basin that fills and empties through the plug-hole and the glass indicator tube in which the liquid rises and falls.

Where a high-pressure squirting action is required, it is often convenient to use the compressed-air type of fire extinguisher. This should be filled to two-thirds of its capacity with water and then pressurised either with an airline or foot-pump.

Ornamental fountains
Conventional pumps and sprays may be used for ornamental fountains in the studio, but the sound of tinkling water often becomes a distraction. To overcome this, the bowl should be lined with felt cloth and the water allowed to drain into a lower receptacle.

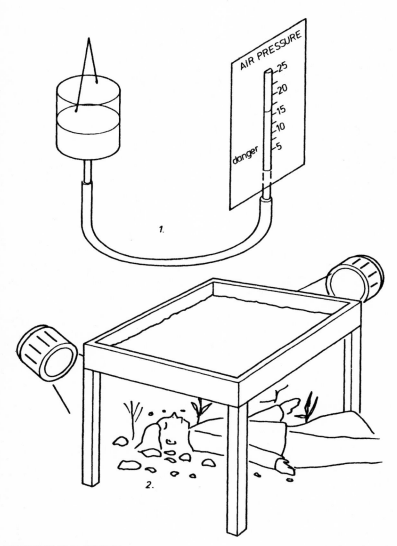

WATER IN THE STUDIO

1. Simulated gauges
The raising and lowering of a water container behind the scenes allows a water-tube gauge to be controlled to very fine limits.

2. Using water trays
A 'drowned person' sequence may be filmed using the real actor if he or she is situated underneath a glass bottomed tray containing water.

73

Dry-Ice Generators

The swirling clouds of white mist used for 'dream sequences' are produced by immersing solid carbon dioxide (dry ice) in hot water. The resulting clouds are a mixture of water vapour and liberated carbon dioxide gas.

Simple generation
Solid carbon dioxide is supplied in conveniently-sized blocks that can be broken up with a hammer. Dropped into hot water the pieces produce copious clouds of vapour, but in doing so make an audible bubbling noise. As it gives off its heat, the water quickly cools and turns to ice. The effect diminishes in proportion with the lowering temperature.

Controlled generation
A well designed and constructed generator avoids cooling-off problems. The water is heated electrically and its temperature is thermostatically maintained throughout the operation. Generation takes place within a box with good thermal insulation that also helps to reduce the noise level. The broken dry ice, contained in a wire basket, is lowered into the hot water when the effect is required. Lifting it out causes the effect to stop. A small fan positioned above water level can be switched on to assist the distribution of the mist, which is sometimes ducted away in large-bore flexible pipes.

Operational notes
The water vapour eventually condenses back into water. The area around the generator can therefore get quite wet if the machine is run for long periods. Carbon dioxide is not a poisonous gas, but when it collects in low lying areas it excludes the air. The possibility of asphyxiation must be anticipated where scenes include low-lying enclosed sets and where performers have to lie down in the mist.

Very hot water causes the clouds to rise. Cooler water keeps them down.

Where large areas are being covered in mist it is helpful to surround the area with two-foot-high retaining walls. Scenic flats are suitable.

Some attention should be paid to the necessity for siting dry-ice generators where they can replenish the effect with the minimum of intrusion. The fairy glade loses its aura of quiet enchantment if dry-ice clouds can be seen belting in from one side of the set. Sympathetic direction can help if cameras pick out different parts of the set while others are being replenished.

Dry ice should not be handled with bare hands.

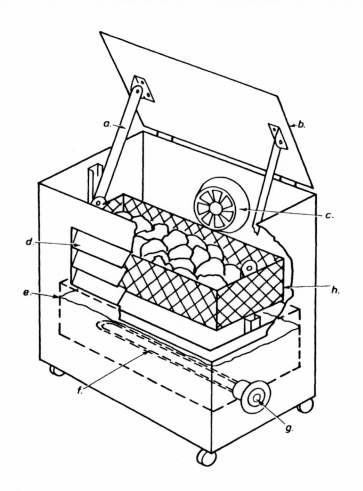

DRY-ICE GENERATOR

A typical dry-ice machine used in film and television studios. a, Lowering arm.
b, Operating lid. c, Booster fan (use optional). d, Outlet louvres. e, Thermally-insulated
water trough. f, Water heater. g, Thermostat. h, Wire basket containing dry ice.

Radar and Oscilloscopes

A practical commercial radar display requires a signal from a rotating aerial to produce a picture on the cathode-ray tube. It is, therefore, seldom possible to use fully practical radar equipment in studio productions.

Radar scanner

To simulate a working radar it is possible to have a 'display' which is scanned by a rotating radial 'beam' of light. This can be achieved by using a rotating disc of clear plastic sprayed with black paint in such a way that it fades gradually from clear to opaque. The opaque section should cover at least one third of the disc, while the clear area should be in the form of a narrow line.

The disc is fitted to the extended spindle of a gear box driven by an electric motor. Alternatively it can be driven by a motor via belts and pulleys.

In front of the disc is the display. This is also a sheet of clear plastic sprayed uniformly with black paint to render it opaque. The display (usually in the form of a map) is scratched through the paint leaving a clear, brilliant outline. Next comes a sheet of tracing paper and finally another sheet of clear plastic.

A light placed behind the disc provides a typical rotational scan followed by the characteristic fade out. The effect is enhanced by putting a yellow or blue-green gel in front of the display.

Where 'moving' blips are required a number of clear areas can be covered and uncovered in turn by pulling sliders behind the main display disc. This activity is carried out during the period when the area is blacked out.

Oscillographs

Oscilloscope patterns, provided that they do not have to show varying patterns, can be simulated with a double mirror partially sprayed on both sides with black paint. The paint is sprayed in such a way as to fade out the trailing edge of both mirrors.

A light reflecting from the rotating mirrors falls on a display which has been prepared by spraying clear plastic with black paint and then scratching out the area required for the simulated trace. The front is covered with tracing paper and coloured gel.

Mock traces

A motorised, revolving bent wire, painted white and set in a black hole gives the impression of a realistic trace if not seen too closely. A useful gimmick for science-fiction sets.

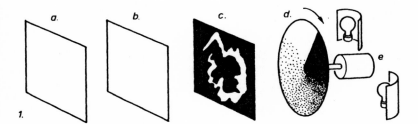

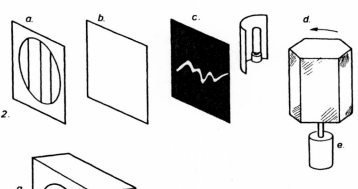

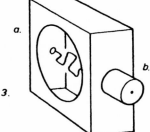

RADAR AND OSCILLOSCOPES

1. Parts for a motorised radar scan simulator
a, Clear plastic front. b, Diffuser screen. c, Clear plastic with scan pattern.
d, Graduated disc. e, Motor.

2. Parts for a simulated oscilloscope display
a, Clear plastic front. b, Diffuser screen. c, Clear plastic with trace pattern. d, Mirror
drum. e, Motor.

3. A 'busy' display to use in the background
a, White painted bent wire in black box. b, Motor.

Laboratory and Chemical Effects

Laboratory sets are either comedic or semi-practical. In both cases, unless they are required simply for dressing, something must be seen to happen. In the comedy arrangement it is usually sufficient to fill a few chemical flasks with brightly coloured liquids and to prime them with small pieces of dry ice prior to a take. But for implied realism more subtle effects are required.

Chemical equipment
A suitable arrangement of chemical flasks, glass tubes and rubber hoses can be made to work automatically if a piece of dry-ice is placed in a flask of warm water connected to the system. The released carbon dioxide bubbling along the various glass tubes makes the whole thing appear busy. Colouring of the water in the tubes can be achieved by using soluble food dyes.

Compressed air introduced into the bottom of a glass column of liquid gives an impressive bubble display.

Steam from a small boiler or electric kettle conducted over a container of dry-ice gives the effect of acid fumes leaking away.

Chemical reactions
Carbon tetrachloride poured onto expanded polystyrene dissolves it rapidly. The polystyrene can be finished to resemble such materials as paper, minerals, metals, wood or even flesh.

Titanium tetrachloride poured on clothing or thrown on a floor in a test tube or flask fumes rapidly, resembling the most dangerous acid.

By mixing acetic acid with cyclohexylamine, fumes are produced that resemble light smoke or 'steam'.

A solution of potassium permanganate in water produces a browny mauve liquid (not unlike some wines). It clears if a solution of hypo is added.

Invisible writing or marks on paper or cloth appear on cue if they are written with a solution of sodium salicylate. Application of a solution of iron sulphate or ferric chloride turns the marks brown.

Most carbonated soft drinks fizz animatedly if free sugar is added.

Solutions of bicarbonate of soda and tartaric acid foam if mixed.

WARNING. Many chemicals are hazardous to human health. Check with experts before using or storing.

Titanium tetrachloride is corrosive and toxic, and the fumes should never be inhaled. It should not be allowed to come into contact with the skin.

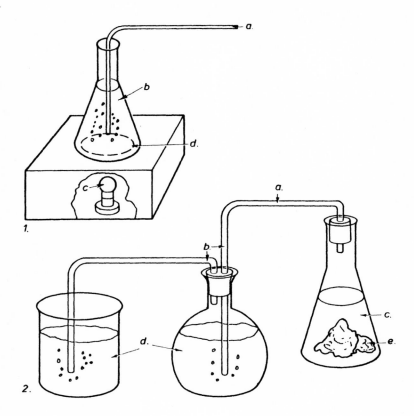

LABORATORY AND CHEMICAL EFFECTS

1. Bubbles
Compressed air blown into a flask makes an impressive bubble display. a,
Compressed air. b, Coloured liquid. c, Lamp. d, Cut-out in box.

2. Laboratory scene
A busy looking display can be created by placing dry-ice in warm water in a flask
connected to a system of tubes and containers. a, Carbon dioxide gas travels along
the tube. b, Glass tubes. c, Warm water. d, Coloured liquid. e, Dry-ice.

Ray Guns and Blasters

Science fiction weapons conventionally demand more visual effects than ordinary hand guns, often being required to emit a beam of 'energy'. The targets also differ from normal in that the rays do not terminate in pools of blood, but instead, generate effects ranging from wholesale mayhem to a few vicious sparks.

Weapons
The designs of ray guns and blasters differ from traditional hand guns in that they are usually bigger and have more external detail. Early examples were fitted with smoke effects and light flashing units, but these have been dropped in favour of smooth laser-type beams of light.

Ray effects
Yet another example of computer-generated effects, these rays are invariably added as a post-production operation. Applied in this way they can be made to move with the weapon, sweep in arcs and produce whatever destructive effect is considered appropriate.

Static ray
An early technique which might assist videomakers is one in which a black stencil containing a cut-out beam is super-imposed on a fixed weapon via the fifty-fifty mirror (page 26). When the two are lined up it is a simple matter to flash or sweep a light behind the stencil.

Target
Most ray-gun effects look good if the target erupts in a very conventional explosion. Methods of providing these are given on pages 102–110.

A further method of achieving a blast effect is to produce the blasted area in advance and then cover it with a removable membrane. For example, a cupboard door that has to be seared by the fearsome blast can be made of wood and the area required to be blasted hacked out with a chisel. Painted black and grey, a suitably devastated effect is implied. The treated door is then covered with self-adhesive wood-grain plastic sheet to make it look new.

To explode the area, a measure of gunpowder is applied to the sticky backing of the wood grain sheet before application, and a pyrofuse inserted through the back of the door to ignite it. The resultant explosion burns the sheet and blows it outward in a satisfactory searing effect.

RAY GUNS AND BLASTERS

1. Prepared damage
Expanded polystyrene gives a melted blast effect. This hole will then be provided with a small amount of gunpowder and a pyrofuse before being covered with self-adhesive vinyl sheet.

2. Zapped!
This is the result when the 'wooden' panel is supposedly hit by a blaster's high-energy beam.

Robots and Monsters

Robots and monsters are usually designed to be operated remotely. Some famous science fiction creatures have required a whole team of people pulling levers, pressing switches and calling commands to function for just a few seconds.

Eyes
The eyes play a significant part in establishing the role of these characters and certain designs have become traditional. Metallic robots may require no more than slits which light up, flash or send out deadly rays. Creatures and humanoid figures need human-like eyes.

For these the surgical glass eyes used to replace human ones can be incorporated in the design; they look so real that the viewer is tempted to believe that the creatures are alive.

Eyeballs
Table tennis balls are invariably used for non-humanoid eyes, particularly where they are required to move. To do this they must be mounted on a gimbal, which will permit them to swivel from side to side and move up and down.

Bowden cables or spring-return nylon lines can be employed to control the various movements.

Eyelids can be made to move if they are constructed of thin latex attached to a half-ring which swivels on the same axis as the ball.

The mouth
It is not easy to create realistic lip and mouth movements, especially if they have to be synchronised with speech. Usually an up and down movement of the jaw must suffice.

Flexible latex incorporating a hinged metal jaw can be built into a solid head and, if articulated by pneumatic or hydraulic controls, will respond with reasonable mobility. Where feasible it is better to use an operator's hand.

Other movements
Heads that turn and arms that lift can be actuated by electric motors. Should these be difficult to obtain they can be stripped from various domestic appliances, which also provide a wide range of belts, pulleys, chains, sprockets and gears.

Car accessories (wipers, heater fans, electric aerials, etc.) provide a rich source of low-voltage motors and drives. Few of them run silently, however.

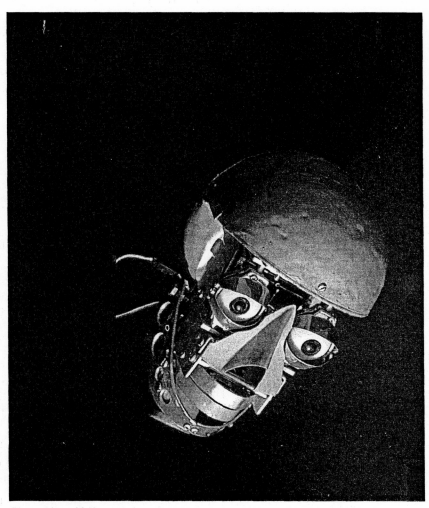

Photo: Merry Motion

ROBOTS AND MONSTERS

A robot head constructed from metal and fibreglass. The eyes which move from side to side and up and down are made from plastic balls into which have been inserted the eyes from a teddy bear. Top and bottom eyelids are articulated and the bottom jaw moves up and down.

When finished this metal unit will be covered by a rubber face mask and dressed with eyelashes and a wig.

83

The Smoke Gun

Smoke that can be turned on and off when needed is an essential requirement for the making of television programmes. Generated in special devices known as smoke guns (although terms such as smoke machine and smoke generator are also used), they are heated either electrically or by gas.

Most of these devices employ a common principle: smoke fluid is passed through a small bore tube or restricted passage which is heated to a critical temperature. The super-heated fluid, which is pressurised, emerges from a nozzle, vaporising into white smoke.

Although this is the basic principle, there are other important features which must be incorporated in the design before any smoke gun can work efficiently and safely. Thermostats, pressure by-pass pipes and indicator lights are just some of the features.

Studio guns
Most studio smoke guns are electrically heated which means they are tethered to a mains supply. However, this is not unduly restrictive because the heat exchanger is provided with a heat retaining block which enables the gun to be disconnected and carried around for several minutes after disconnection. Usually, however, an extended mains lead is used.

Gas guns
Hand-held guns working from small camping-gas cylinders work on a similar principle, but are ignited by match or spark. They must be turned off immediately after use to protect the heat exchanger coil from burning out. This limits their use for short intermittent bursts.

Outdoor smoke machines
Again, the principle is the same, but these devices have a very large coil heated by a gas burner fed with bottled propane. Pressurisation is achieved by hand-pumping air into the fluid container.

Using the smoke gun
In the majority of cases, smoke guns are used to create foggy atmospheres or fire scenes. For these they are either set down on the studio floor and allowed to run, or picked up and carried about. Other requirements, however, demand that they be supplied with hoses to produce a point source of smoke or spreaders to direct it under a door. However, smoke fluid, when cooled, condenses back to liquid so additions to the nozzle end must be kept short. Smoke guns should never be pointed directly at any part of the body.

1. A smoke gun designed for use in TV and movie studios
Equipment for studio work must be portable and easy to handle.

2. The right equipment for the job
Large special effects departments are able to call upon a range or indoor and outdoor smoke guns.

85

Pyrotechnic and other Smokes

Pyrotechnic smoke is produced by igniting a slow-burning chemical mixture in a container which inhibits the rate of flame spread and ensures that the mixture receives no additional oxygen from outside. Thus, combustion is made as inefficient as possible and smoke is created. The mixture usually contains various smoke-producing agents such as naphthalene or bitumen, etc.

For smoke to be produced it is essential that the mixture does not flame. Smoke pots should not therefore be placed in proximity to anything that will catch fire, so igniting the smoke at the mouth of the pyrotechnic.

Charcoal smoke

Tablets used for the burning of incense in swinging censors for religious ceremonies can be used for smoke effects in the studio. Lit and placed on fireproof surfaces, or in shallow tins, they glow red-hot for about thirty minutes. In that state they produce no smoke, but if a few drops of machine oil are applied to the central unlit portion of charcoal a considerable amount of grey smoke is produced. This effect will last, diminishing gradually, until all the oil is used up. Barbecue charcoal briquettes can be used in a similar manner. Tablets or briquettes of this type are useful for all sorts of local effects which need to work without attention. Placed in fireplaces they add to the realism of the studio gas fires, while positioned around a set they give a vivid impression of a smokey night-club or a busy, industrial scene. They can be placed in studio chimneys required to smoke for long periods and also serve to authenticate camp fires that are illuminated from within by electric lights.

Burning food in cooking scenes may be simulated by placing a charcoal tablet under the incinerated items.

Hot-wire smoke

Occasionally it is required to produce an instant smoke effect where it is impractical to run a pipe from a smoke gun or to employ pyrotechnics. An answer to this situation is to use a short piece of nickel-chrome wire (the sort used in electric fire elements) which becomes red-hot when supplied with low-voltage current from a transformer or car battery. The wire should be wrapped around rock wool or glass fibre impregnated with machine oil. When switched on the hot wire quickly causes the oil to smoke (although if too hot the oil will burst into flames). This technique has many applications, among which are smoking trousers and 'electrical equipment' which has to be seen to have some sort of dramatic short circuit or electric malfunction.

PYROTECHNIC AND OTHER SMOKES

1. A burning compressed-charcoal tablet gives off smoke when a few drops of oil are applied.
2. Principle of the heated steel wire encased in oil-impregnated rock wool.
3. A charcoal tablet being used to imply that food is burning.
4. The hot wire being used to simulate an overheated cable.
5. Some pyrotechnic smoke-pots are electrically fired, others have ignitable fuses.
6. Pyrotechnic smoke pots being used for location fire effect.

87

Flames

The amount of flame permitted in a TV studio is limited. Expensive floors, fire alarms and sprinkler systems restrict its use. Nevertheless by employing lighting effects, smoke and controllable flames it is possible to create realistic fire sequences.

Flame forks
Made from metal tubes these can be constructed in fan shapes or as tubes with drilled holes. Coupled by industrial-rubber hoses to a bottled gas supply they are used to provide controllable flame wherever required. To obviate the risk of flash-over it is wise to have each flame fork ignited by an operator only as it is turned on. If this is not practical, it is feasible to have smaller pilot jets independently fed and positioned below the main flame forks.

Flame drum
For some years the effect of flickering flames was achieved by shining a powerful light through a revolving drum of clear plastic on which had been painted sloping black lines. The effect of the lines criss-crossing each other produced an upward flickering movement which looked quite convincing.

Lighting effects
Lamps with revolving discs (gobos) which give a variety of effects are now universally available. The flame effects are, like the flame drum, mechanical but acceptable. Better are the effects created by runs of lights that travel sequentially. Using two or more lines operating at different frequencies, these produce a random effect that is nearly perfect.

Flaming brands
These should be made of an incombustible material (fireproofed wood is permissible) to which has been attached bound cotton waste. The business end should be soaked in kerosene and allowed to stand upside down until all free liquid has drained off. Metal handles should not be used because they transmit heat.

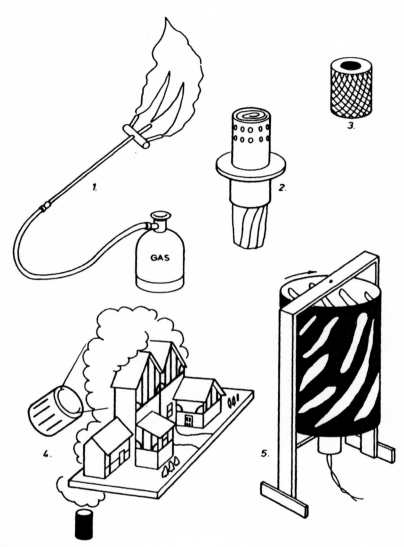

FLAMES

Practical flames can be introduced anywhere in the set if flame-forks (1) are used. Their effects can be heightened by using the flame-drum (5), a rotating cylinder of clear plastic on which is painted sloping shadows. A lamp shone through the drum produces cross-modulation of the clear patches, giving the effect of flames wreathing upward. For hand-held torches (2), impregnated cotton waste may be packed into a short length of metal tube. An alternative head (3) comprises a thick stump of candle set inside a cylindrical lamp-wick. Back lit smoke (4) can seem to be a fierce conflagration when used with models.

Fire Effects in the Studio

A studio 'conflagration' is composed more of reflected light and smoke than actual flame – in fact some sequences have been recorded without any flame at all. Nevertheless by using a suitable combination of all three, it is easy to create very dramatic fire scenes. Controlled by switches and gas taps, fire effects of this kind can be turned on and off at will – only the smoke has a lingering persistence.

Because fire scenes are best arranged to favour a single viewpoint it is often necessary to re-dress the scene whenever there is a change of angle. When this is done it is important to recognise the need for smoke continuity.

Use of flame forks
Flame forks (page 88) positioned below the camera can be manipulated to provide a significant amount of flame, particularly when the forks are gently agitated by hand. Unfortunately this 'frontal flame' ploy has become something of a cliché and care should be taken when using it.

If flame forks are made from soft copper, they can be bent to adapt to the shape of the set.

Small forks strategically positioned in or around furniture can be used without causing damage, but care should be taken that radiant heat does not scorch the fabric or blister paintwork.

Smoke
Smoke is the most important ingredient in a fire scene because apart from the fact that it would be there anyway, it picks up light from the flames and the flicker effects. It should not be allowed to build up to an extent where it would obscure background effects.

Outdoor sets
Erecting a set outdoors imposes much less restraint; real fires and real destruction can be arranged – with the actors having clear passage to areas of safety.

It is sometimes necessary to clad part of the ceiling to retain the smoke which under the influence of rising heat would otherwise be carried away.

In order to work without limitations, producers commonly make use of empty factories and disused buildings to stage fire scenes.

FIRE EFFECTS IN THE STUDIO

1. Smoke lit from a lamp shining through a flame drum. a, Flame drum. b, Smoke machine.
2. Indestructible glass fibre curtains used with flame fork.
3. Flame fork behind furniture.
4. Flame fork in front of camera.
5. Flaming 'furniture shaped' rig being superimposed over real furniture, using fifty/fifty mirror technique. a, Semi-transparent mirror.
6. Pyrotechnic flare being burnt to provide both light and smoke. a, Sand tray.
b, Fireproof sheet (large studios only).

Fire Effects in the Open

Fire sequences outdoors benefit from the fact that materials may be burned freely without too much concern for surrounding areas. At night the light of the fire predominates – in daylight it is the smoke.

Burning buildings
Where practical buildings are used and it is essential to create the effect of fire without damaging the property, pyrotechnic flares can be laid on trays of sand. These flares produce an intense source of white light and also a considerable amount of light-coloured smoke. The combination gives the effect of a large conflagration.

For night shots a few flares should be positioned at the back of the building to silhouette its shape against the night sky.

Flame arks
Burning material, however combustible, if placed on the ground gives flames of only limited height. To increase the effect it is necessary to get as much air to as large a burning surface as possible.

A frame shaped like a pitched roof and covered with chicken wire provides an optimum arrangement for good combustion. Kerosene-saturated sacking or cloth is laid over the chicken wire and ignited from the bottom. Air is able to reach both sides of the burning material which is supported by the frame until burnt out.

An ark may be positioned behind small buildings or foreground vehicles to give dramatic effects with safety.

Petrogel
If gasoline is mixed with various agents it can be made thick enough to apply to the surfaces of doors and walls to provide local flame to supplement larger effects. Petrogel is a mixture of thixotrophic powder and gasoline.

Certain industrial adhesives are in themselves inflammable and may be thinned with gasoline to provide a sticky combustible material that will burn without dripping or running.

WARNING: Be sensible!

Place fire extinguishers and buckets of water close to the sources of fire effects.

Make sure that all personnel involved have free access to safety before igniting effects.

Remember that a building full of smoke can endanger the lives of people in areas not directly involved in the fire sequence.

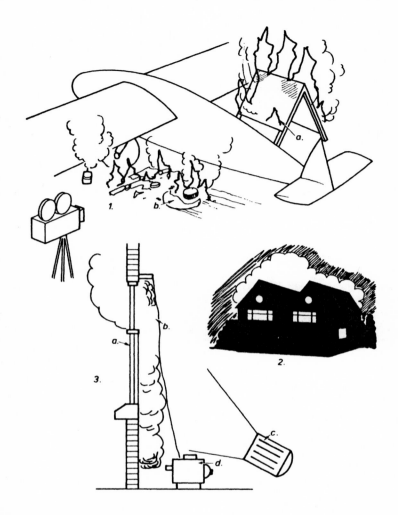

FIRE EFFECTS IN THE OPEN

1. Wreckage
A burning aircraft can be simulated by using large flames with small pieces of burning wreckage scattered in the foreground. a, Flame ark. b, Burning pieces in foreground.

2. Burning buildings
Back-lit smoke at the rear of a building gives a good effect at night.

3. Burning rooms
Burning rooms can be suggested by using smoke and light. a, Half-open window. b, Polythene sheet. c, Lamp. d, Smoke gun.

93

Fires and Furnaces

Open fires in the studio consist mostly of logs set in large baronial fire-places or coal in old-fashioned fire grates. Both need to display practical flames and, sometimes, smoke, but generally they are fuelled by gas with the flames controlled to remain constant throughout the recording.

Open fires
A prerequisite for any open fire is its fuel. Logs, coal, twigs and even blocks of peat can be made from plaster of Paris applied to wire formers. Painted with water-based paint, these will eventually deteriorate where they are subjected to heat, but, nevertheless, will last for many hours. Ceramic logs and imitation coal are commercially available from the manufacturers of domestic gas fires.

The gas burners may be constructed of copper tubes that sit between the logs, or placed below a bed of sand where a more dispersed area of flame results. In the unlikely event that bottled gas is unavailable, domestic fire lighters can be used – although they must be constantly replenished.

Smoke can be supplied by charcoal tablets or incense.

Actions
Actions in which letters or papers are thrown onto a gas-fuelled open fire are normally permissible – the burning seldom lasts long enough to endanger the set, but such actions as using a poker or replenishing the logs or coal are best avoided.

Furnaces and red-hot coals
For braziers, furnaces and stoves, it is possible to use an electric lamp surrounded by glass fibre. Some varieties of this material are available in a suitable pink/orange hue, but white varieties may be tinted with spirit-based dyes. Alternatively, the light source may be coloured.

Dobs of black and grey paint applied to the outside layers of the glass-fibre add realism. Flames are not usually required for this type of fire, but smoke can be used as above.

FIRES AND FURNACES

1. A brazier constructed of glass fibre with internal lighting and a charcoal smoke unit.
a, Glass fibre. b, Lamp. c, Charcoal tablet.
2. Log fire using piped gas and charcoal tablet.
3. Non-combustible log with flames fed by gas dispersed in a sand tray. a, Log made from plaster-covered chicken wire. b, Sand. c, Gas.
4. Augmented fire effect using flame drum to supply illumination.

Hot and Molten Metal

It is often difficult to show that something being used in a production is supposed to be hot. Branding irons or torture implements used in dark dramatic scenes need internal illumination. To seem convincing they must emit light and illuminate items with which they come into contact. Clear acrylic plastic transmits light so it can be used to make articles in which a light source at one end illuminates the other.

Pokers
The business end of a red-hot poker can be mocked-up by constructing it from tinted clear plastic into which has been inserted a small bulb. There is, however, a fluorescent acrylic plastic that needs no internal light to look red-hot. If the ends are provided with smoke by using the hot-wire method outlined on page 86 they appear suitably convincing.

A felt-pad treated with liquid make-up and secreted at the back of the red-hot poker produces nasty looking burns on human flesh.

Pouring molten metal
Water with finely powdered aluminium sprinkled on its surface can pass as molten lead. Similarly, brass powder appears as molten gold. Such liquids can be poured, but look unconvincing without the addition of smoke.

A realistic effect of molten metal is achieved if the liquid is contained in a special crucible with a transparent bottom of plastic or glass. Light directed from below makes the 'metal' appear to be red-hot when the surface of powder is stirred or disturbed. Small pieces of floating cork add to the realism by appearing as slag.

Flat iron
A flat iron that has to scorch cloth can have the sole-plate smeared with brown grease-paint. Smoke produced within the iron by the hot wire method can be made to emerge from small holes around the bottom.

Use of heated items
The fact that safety in the studio is of paramount importance often leads effects designers to go to extraordinary lengths to simulate even the most mundane activity. Red-hot metal being quenched in water is a typical example. In such cases it is wise to consider using the real thing. The alternative is to screen something which looks less than realistic and is much more expensive.

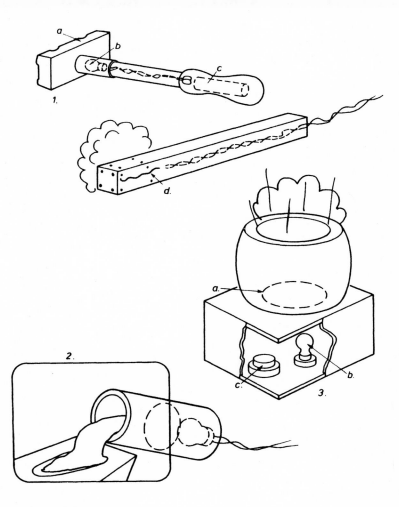

HOT AND MOLTEN METAL

1. Branding irons
Red-hot pokers, branding irons, etc. must emit light and sometimes smoke.
a, Fluorescent plastic. b, Lamp. c, Battery. d, Hot wire smoke.

2. Pouring molten metal
Water poured from a pot with a transparent bottom and built-in lamp. Even when poured the water continues to transmit light.

3. Simulated hot metal
The metal itself is never seen, but the light and the smoke arising imply that hot metal is contained within. a, Open base. b, Lamp. c, Charcoal tablet.

Explosives

Gunpowder (or 'black powder') is a pyrotechnic mixture which burns at an extremely fast rate. This rate increases under pressure so that, when confined, gunpowder literally explodes. This is known as a deflagration.

The more powerful high-explosive materials are said to detonate, which is a different effect altogether and is brought about by the de-stabilisation of molecular structures. High explosives do not need to be confined, nor do they respond to initiation by fire. They must be triggered by small devices called detonators, which deliver a powerful shock setting off the process of de-stabilisation.

Their use

The majority of war scenes recorded outdoors rely on pyrotechnics for their explosions. However, there are occasions when something more powerful is required, and this is when high explosives are employed. Examples would include a huge underwater eruption to simulate the detonation of a sea-mine, the impact of a torpedo, a boat which had to be blown up on water, or, on land, a real building which had to be totally demolished.

Some ground effects can benefit from the use of high-explosive materials, as these give a sharper impact than pyrotechnics. An aerial attack with missiles might come into this category.

High explosives have other uses. An effects expert would have little choice but to use them when faced with the problem of blowing a branch from a tree or demolishing a number of wooden supports to drop a bridge.

The suppliers of these materials publish specifications and instructions which can be obtained on request, but all users in the entertainment industry must be fully trained and must hold both a certificate of competence and a valid user licence.

Types

High explosives for film use come in several varieties. Some are in the form of loose material, and others resemble putty, but one of the most useful for smaller effects comes as a reel of cord which can be cut into lengths. All require their appropriate detonators.

Regulations

Quite obviously, stringent regulations govern the purchase, use and storage of these materials. People who need them for TV or movie-making purposes are advised to consult both the appropriate licensing authority and the local police.

DO'S AND DONT'S

Accidents seldom happen without human participation; they result from carelessness or diminished concentration.

DO ensure that all containers of explosive or incendiary materials are kept covered at all times.

DON'T make up large amounts of material nor work with anything but the minimum of ingredients.

DO ensure that unused, non stock, items are destroyed at the end of a programme.

DON'T destroy by ignition. Gunpowder and flashpowder should be neutralised in water.

DO wear protective goggles when working with explosives.

DON'T connect anything to wires before ensuring that they are disconnected from any form of power supply.

DO rehearse dangerous effects and check results before using them near people.

DON'T hurry or take chances. Don't revise explosive or fire effects without further rehearsal.

DO expect the unexpected.

EXPLOSIVES

Firing Boxes and Exploders

Commercial exploders can be purchased, but for effects work it is often better to use purpose-built devices.

Uses
Firing boxes are used mainly to fire pyrotechnics, explosives and bullet-hits, but they are also used to operate such things as panel lights, dropping boxes, remotely operated props and many other things. Used with long runs of cable they should be capable of supplying a voltage sufficiently high to overcome the resistance of the wire.

Facilities
Designs should include a rotary switch for rapid-sequence operations as well as single buttons for individual items. A permanent, transparent, plastic cover fitted over the buttons allows them to be used freely, but prevents the entry of dirt and grit.

Robust, easy to use terminals should be incorporated and situated as far apart as practicable.

Danger points
Toggle switches that may be inadvertently left in the 'on' position should *never* be used, but remember that grit and sand can jam push buttons in the 'on' position.

A separate battery supply, to be connected only at the last moment, safeguards the person wiring the charges. To make absolutely sure that it is not connected, *he* can carry it with him.

Indicator lamp circuits should be carefully designed so that they do not provide a secondary path to the terminals.

Circuits
If a firing box operates on a low-voltage high current, it is advisable to fire detonators or pyrofuses on a parallel circuit. If a commercial exploder, incorporating a high-voltage magneto, is used then the items may be wired in series.

Nail board
Entirely primitive, the nail-board still turns up from time to time. It has several virtues; it is simple, the circuit can be plainly seen and the speed of operation is easy to control.

A nail-board is a length of wood into which has been driven a row of nails with about an inch and a half of nail left protruding. Wires soldered to each nail are taken to the pyrotechnics or bullet hits and these are fired by wiping the common return lead along the row of nails.

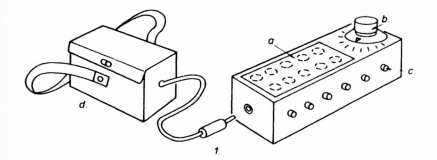

1.

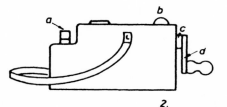

2.

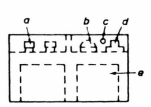

3.

FIRING BOXES AND EXPLODERS

1. General purpose firing box
The battery supply is detachable and can be carried by the person wiring up the charges. Not suitable for very long cable runs. a, Press buttons behind plastic shield. b, Rotary switch. c, Terminals. d, Battery case.

2. High-voltage magneto type
Fires one circuit only, but suitable for long distance work with a large number of charges wired in series. a, Terminals. b, Pilot light. c, Press button. d, Handle.

3. Simple battery box
A basic type with on/off switch, red indicator light and single press-button to fire one circuit. Ideal for studio work. a, Terminals. b, Pilot light. c, Switch. d, Press button. e, Batteries.

101

Pyrotechnics

Pyrotechnics used in TV and movie-making are obtained from commercial sources or are purpose-made items concocted in the effects workshop. Strict regulations govern their manufacture as well as the premises in which they are stored. Statutory licences must be obtained for both. Even the cutting open of a simple firework can be regarded as 'manufacturing', and the same rules apply.

Stage pyrotechnics
These (and there is a considerable range) are designed to meet the main requirements of the entertainment industry.

They include pyrotechnics which discharge small sparks, produce huge flashes, deliver small bangs and create large explosions. There are various smokes, coloured fire, flash-paper and so on.

The sparking varieties are used to simulate electrical faults, welding sequences and the contact that comes from a speeding vehicle as it grounds on the highway.

Magnesium flash-pots may be used for anything from the appearance of a genie to the searing flash of a bomb blast.

There are also various fuses, simulated grenades, tear gas bombs and other items.

Explosions
Commercially produced bombs and shell-burst simulators are available in a variety of forms, many deriving from army training requirements. Generally only those that are electrically initiated should be considered.

Where possible it is a good idea to fire a number of these items experimentally, recording the results on video or film and noting the way in which they were employed. Records of this kind can be extremely useful when planning productions.

Certain large flashes and bomb simulators may be fired in the bigger studios, but only when special precautions are taken.

PYROTECHNICS

A few of the pyrotechnics, fuses and firing devices used in television productions. The plastic beer-bottle containing gasoline is used for explosive fireball effects. It is initiated by the sealed gunpowder charge immersed in the liquid.

103

Pyrotechnics in the Studio

Any form of fire in a TV or movie studio must be rigorously controlled and constantly monitored. Several huge studios have been totally destroyed because these rules were not observed. Nevertheless viewing audiences do not pay to see regulations – they demand realism and are entitled to be given it. To achieve this safely is the responsibility of the production unit.

Detonators and pyrofuses
Detonators cannot be used to set fire to things, but pyrofuses are designed specifically for this purpose. To ignite gas or inflammable liquids successfully they require a primer – a small amount of flash powder or gunpowder placed around their heads.

Used to ignite gunpowder or flash powder pyrofuses should be buried in the heart of the mixture, ensuring that they are not against the wall of the container. Where this is a polythene bag it is possible for the head of the pyrofuse to fire through the plastic without igniting the contents.

Fireworks
Pyrotechnics are frequently used in the studio, most popular being the small magnesium (or aluminium) flashes associated with magicians' tricks and illusions.

Other fireworks often seen in productions are sparklers, which may be held in the hand, used to simulate slow-burning fuses or set out simply as decorations. They should be initiated by another firework (a port-fire) or a small gas torch; ordinary matches produce insufficient heat and take too long.

The conventional hand-held golden rain firework, when slipped into a welder's torch, can be used to simulate the cutting open of a safe door. A surface of wax applied to the door beforehand enhances the effect.

For a close-up on a safe-cracker's face a sparkler may be held just off camera to imply that cutting is taking place.

For fiesta sequences and dance routines a curtain of fire can be arranged by hanging micagerbs on an overhead line. The golden sparks discharged from these devices are incandescent mica flakes which quickly lose their heat and their power to ignite.

Safety
For *emergency* use it is essential to keep fire extinguishers to hand wherever fire effects are taking place, but for the dowsing of small local fires, spent cases, etc. a pump-up garden spray is more suitable.

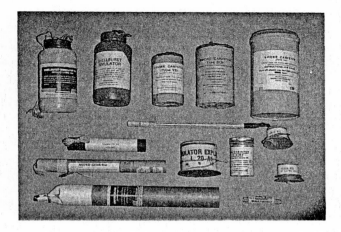

PYROTECHNICS IN THE STUDIO

1. A selection of indoor and outdoor pyrotechnics for professional use.
2. Gas filled balloons can be employed to give a quick burst of flame.

Pyrotechnics in the Open

Mealed gunpowder (or black powder) confined in tough cardboard cases or plastic containers is commonly used for pyrotechnic explosions in the open. There are also several commercial products known as bomb simulators which produce explosions of differing hues. Some have light grey smoke, and others a browny/black.

The mortar
This is a heavy steel tube with one end sealed. Primed with a charge of black powder and loaded with a paper wad and stout wooden dowel, this device is employed to hurl items into the air. It can be used to demolish wooden sheds, tip over piles of drums, fling dummy soldiers over parapets and blast out 'lightweight' tree stumps. The effect is enhanced if secondary, more visual, pyrotechnics are placed around the base of the mortar.

Ground explosions
For the best and safest effects, ground maroons or bomb simulators should be fired in steel pans sunk into the ground. These prevent stones from being flung around like shrapnel. On their own, simulators provide a satisfactory explosion, but their effects can be enhanced by piling peat, cork chips and pieces of builders' softboard on top of them. Placed in between bags of flour they will produce an improved fire-ball effect. For the large fire-balls associated with napalm bombs or exploding automobiles, one or more simulators are placed below plastic bags containing gasoline.

The trip-wire
In order to ensure that ground explosions fire at exactly the right moment and at a safe distance from performing actors, trip-wires are set out in the field through which the actors run. The action must be carefully rehearsed and each actor must traverse only the pre-determined path.

The trip-wire consists of a cord stretched between two tent pegs which when snatched pulls a small piece of insulating plastic from between the jaws of a clothes peg. The jaws, having been fitted with metal contacts, then fire the bomb.

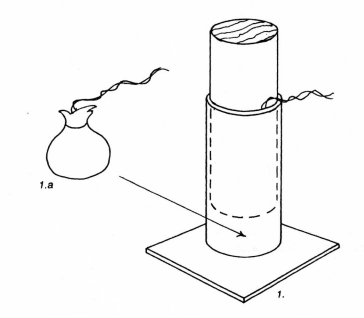

PYROTECHNICS ON LOCATION

1. Steel mortar and wooden plunger used for throwing items into the air or demolishing buildings.

1.a Loosely wrapped gunpowder to eject the plunger. It is essential to place a wad of paper or cloth between the charge and the projectile.

2. Mortar pan used to fire ground bursts and bomb simulators,

Safe Studio Explosions – 1

Using the stored energy in compressed air or elastic rope, harmless and effective explosions can be achieved without resorting to the use of dangerous or impractical explosives.

Whoofer

This is a device consisting of a pressure vessel connected to a funnel-shaped hopper. The storage vessel has an inlet for compressed air and an exhaust valve which releases the air through a large diameter, heavy-walled flexible tube. The exhaust valve is a large capacity quick-release device capable of discharging all the air at once.

The hopper can be filled with powder and debris and it is usual to heap further piles of debris on top of the filled hopper.

A switch coupled to the lever of the valve can be wired to a flashpot positioned by the hopper. This dramatically supplements the effect.

Elasticated explosions

If a cupboard containing a bomb has to explode, simulation can be achieved by making the cupboard from separate components – doors, sides, top, etc. These are assembled on the set where the explosion is to take place.

Heavy-duty nylon threads are then passed through holes in the individual parts and knotted together on the inside. Strong elastic cords tied to the free ends of the nylon are strained back to fixing points. The position of the parts is checked for alignment and small conical wedges pressed into the holes from the inside, trapping the threads firmly in the woodwork. To prevent slip it is advisable to tie knots in the nylon at these junctions.

A flashpot is hung just below the main knot that joins all the threads on the inside and the firing lead is taken to a convenient operating position.

The exploding flash, burning through the nylon, releases all the parts which then fly outwards in a convincing manner.

To enhance the effect from such dummy explosions the nylon threads may be fastened to inanimate objects around the site of the bomb. For example, a suitcase or parcel bomb can be made to release threads which pull chairs, lamps, carpets, etc. from around the blasted area.

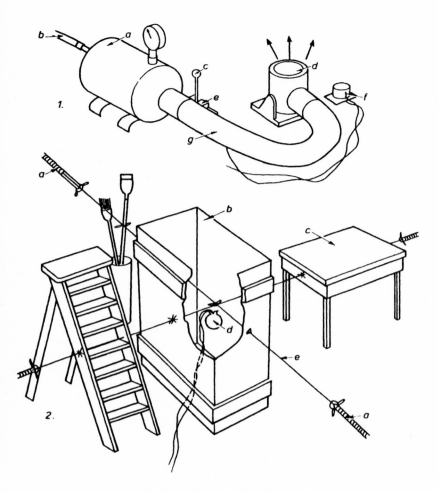

SAFE STUDIO EXPLOSIONS

1. The 'whoofer'
a. Compressed air vessel. b, Input. c, Exhaust valve. d, Discharge pot. e, Switch. f, Flash puff. g, Flexible pipe.

2. Elasticated explosions
a, Elastic. b, Crate in separate parts. c, Lightweight table. d, Flash bomb. e, Nylon cord.

Safe Studio Explosions – 2

Bombs that explode with considerable force and do a great deal of damage are not always easy to simulate in the studio. Nevertheless there are means of achieving very passable results if use is made of large weights to supply the energy.

Swinging weight

A weight tied to a rope and allowed to swing downward in an arc produces equally dramatic results on items that need to fly outward. A door of a room in which a bomb is supposed to have exploded can be fiercely ejected in this way. The weight, held by a solenoid catch, can, when released, sweep down and strike either the top or the bottom of the door. This time a switch fastened on the door itself operates a flash-pot inside the room. It is a good idea to squirt some smoke behind the door just before the action. This improves the effect.

The weight will, of course, enter into shot following the door, so it is necessary to disguise it to look like something that could have been blown from inside the room. If it strikes the bottom of the door its progress can be halted by fixing a second line tied to a dragging sand bag anchor. If it is at the top it can be released from its rope by having a nylon loop which is destroyed by a detonator fired simultaneously with the studio flash.

Falling weight

This arrangement consists simply of a heavy weight which, when released, falls upon the end of a lever. It works very well when applied to items of furniture or free-standing units on the studio floor.

The lever, which usually needs to be hidden, can be positioned either below ground level or inserted through a hole in the scenery.

One example might be a desk situated against a wall. If it were required to be blown to pieces with some force, the lever could be sited behind the scenery, passing through a hole in the set wall and its end locked into the back of the desk. It is easy to see that if the lever passes over a fulcrum then a heavy weight (such as a sandbag) dropped on the other end of the lever will cause the desk to jump up.

To create the explosion a flash-pot could be placed in the desk and fired via a switch fastened to the end of the lever where it would be triggered by the falling weight.

Parts of the desk could be made to fly off by using elastic and nylon lines released as the flashpot burned through the tethering point (see page 160).

110

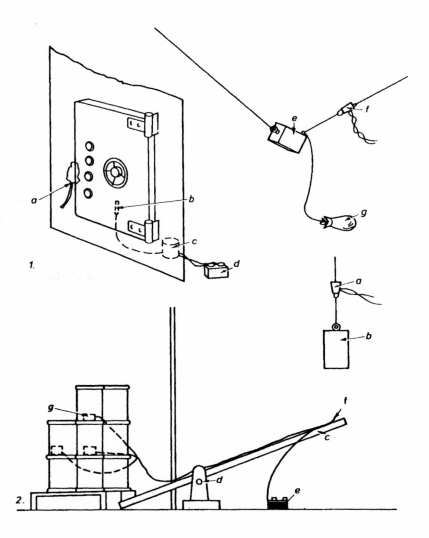

SAFE STUDIO EXPLOSIONS

1. Swinging weight
a, Mock fuse and explosive. b, Switch. c, Flash pot. d, Battery. e, Weight. f, 'Bomb' release. g, Sandbag drag anchor.

2. Falling weight
a, 'Bomb' release. b, Weight. c, Lever. d, Fulcrum. e, Battery. f, Switch. g, Flash pots.

111

Pyrofuses and Bullet Hits

These are small devices fired from a low-voltage electric source. They are similar in size and shape and it is important to know which is which and to ensure that they are used *only* for their stipulated purposes.

Pyrofuses
Pyrofuses are used to ignite pyrotechnic mixtures and flammable substances.

The ignition effect derives from a small bead of chemical material which flares like a match-head when an electric current is passed through an embedded fuse-wire. This is sufficient to ignite such loose materials as mealed gunpowder or flash powder, but is too short-lived to ignite paper or cloth. For these it is necessary to prime the area around the head of the pyrofuse with gunpowder or to treat the material with an area of flammable spirit.

As well as providing ignition the pyrofuse can be used to burn through nylon threads, which in turn can release heavy objects. Fine nylon lines placed close to the head of a pyrofuse will melt instantly, but tougher lines require a priming of gunpowder.

Bullet hits
These are plastic-cased explosive detonators and are usually supplied in full-strength and half-strength grades. They are employed primarily to simulate realistic bullet hits on woodwork, rock faces, bottles and clothing.

Bullet hits discharge small pieces of their tough plastic cases with considerable force, and it is important to ensure that they are suitably shielded when used near actors and studio personnel. Where it is impractical to use rigid shields it is possible to surround the bullet hits with energy-absorbing soft materials such as cloth or plastic foam. Such precautions are usually only necessary when bullet hits are employed on the body.

Circuit test
Where long runs of wire or complicated distributions have several connections it is useful to test the circuits for continuity beforehand. To do this using a standard test meter with an internal battery would be to risk firing the charges. Instead, an approved ohm meter designed for use with explosives must be used.

Pyrofuse.

Plastic cased detonator or bullet-hit.

Metal-cased detonator.

Pyrofuses should always be positioned where they will be in contact with combustible material.

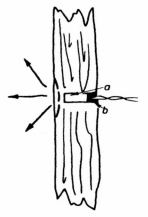

Bullet-hit embedded in wood just under the surface. a, Bullet-hit. b, Wood or clay plug.

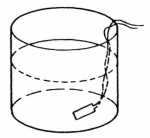

113

Bullet Effects in Scenery

Walls and stonework in the studio are of different materials, and pose different problems, from those used on location.

Walls

The walls in the studio are scenic flats surfaced with artificial brickwork, plaster or wallpaper and are not thick enough to permit realistic effects. The areas in which bullet holes are to appear are therefore backed with blocks of wood in which the holes can be sculpted in advance and then filled with powder and chips and covered with fresh surfacing material. The holes can subsequently be blasted out with plastic bullet hits or pyrofuses fitted with capsules of black powder. An alternative method is to fix steel tubes to the backs of flats.

The type of wall surface is very important. Large plain areas make it difficult to disguise the treated spots whereas unduly busy or patterned surfaces can almost hide the final bullet holes. On location, if an outdoor wall must remain free from damage, it can have false work modelled on the surface with modelling clay. A small pocket of dust provides sufficient effect.

Rocks

Both real and artificial rocks can be treated similarly. First a prepared hole is made on the surface then the bullet hit is laid in the depression. The leads should be cemented to the surface if they are not to fly up when the effect is fired. They can be covered in modelling clay to disguise their whereabouts. The depression should be filled in with powder and chips and smoothed to the original contours. As it is easier to colour the rock than to disguise the prepared hole, suitably blended coloured powders should be dusted liberally all over the area until the holes disappear.

Woodwork

Wood presents fewer problems than other materials as it splits realistically when subjected to the explosive force of a bullet-hit detonator. Two holes, one to accommodate the detonator and one for the wires, are drilled in softwood and the hole is then plugged and disguised.

Direction

Bullet effects often appear far too contrived. To give maximum value for money they tend to run in a straight line up the middle of the frame. It is often easier and more effective to position them erratically in less exposed areas.

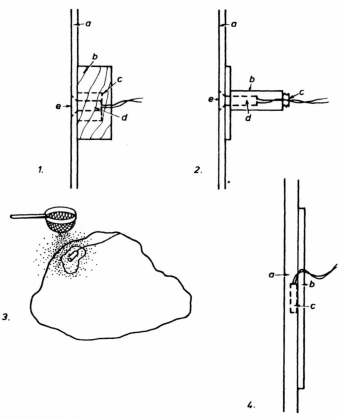

BULLET EFFECTS IN SCENERY

1. Holes in walls
Scenic flats are not thick enough for realistic effects, so the bullet hole area is usually backed with a wood block. a, Scenic flat. b, Wood block. c, Powder. d, Half charge bullet hit. e, Prepared area surfaced with paper.

2. An alternative
A steel tube can be used instead of a wood block. a, Scenic flat. b, Steel tube. c, Screw-in plug. d, Bullet hit. e, Prepared area surfaced with paper.

3. Bullet-struck rocks
A prepared hole takes the bullet hit which is covered with chips and powder.

4. Replacement panels
If, because of rehearsal requirements, the same areas have to be used several times a method must be chosen whereby the holes can be made good by re-papering or by the replacement of suitable panels. a, Replacement panel of timber or board. b, Metal plate. c, Bullet hit.

115

Bullet Effects on Vases and Bottles

While the majority of porcelain or earthenware vases shatter easily when hit with a metal projectile, glass bottles often prove stubbornly indestructible. It is advisable therefore when bottles have to be shot at to use imitations made from other materials. Both wax and plaster react well, but where the action involves a person in close proximity to the bottle, it is safer to use wax.

Using projectiles

Bottles and vases may be destroyed by firing solid projectiles from the capsule gun (page 122). Accurately lined up on the centre of the target the gun should be positioned as near as possible, bearing in mind that the projectile might ricochet from the set behind.

Wax bottles tend to soften in the warmth of a studio. This inhibits the shattering effect, the bullet passing straight through and leaving a hole that is disappointingly un-dramatic. Chilling on a block of dry ice or in a refrigerator helps, as also does filling with cold water.

Vases and bottles made of clear resin of the type used for breakaway glass give the best results, but these usually have to be specially made and are more expensive.

Using detonators

Bullet hit plastic detonators may be used to give realistic bullet effects on vases and bottles whether made from breakaway glass, plaster or wax. It is usual to fill the vessel with liquid and immerse the detonator (suitably waterproofed) in the centre of the liquid. This gives a better pictorial effect, and helps to spread the explosive shock.

In vases of flowers the wires from the detonator may be hidden in the stalks and leaves of the blooms, but with bottles the leads should be taken through a small hole low down in the back.

A simpler method is to situate the detonators under the bottles, hidden in the table or shelf on which the items stand. Success depends on having liquid in the vessels to spread the shock.

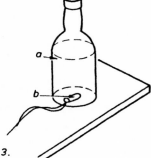

BULLET EFFECT ON VASES AND BOTTLES

1. Exploded from inside
a, Water. b, Waterproofed bullet hit. The water spreads the explosive effect.

2. Mechanical shattering
Where explosives cannot be used, a rapidly moving spring arm can be used as a projectile.

3. External bullet hit
a, Water. b, Bullet hit hidden in shelf.

117

Bullet Effects in Glass and Mirrors

Bullets fired at glass should ideally produce holes surrounded by a number of radiating cracks giving a roughly circular, fist-sized area of destruction. Without this surrounding area of damage, bullet holes appear unconvincing.

Bullet effect by editing
Dramatic effects can be obtained by painting simulated bullet holes on cut-out pieces of self-adhesive clear plastic sheet. When the scene is filmed these cut-outs are applied in sequence to the glass and the resultant film edited to show the holes appearing one after another. With post-dubbed sound-effects this is an economical way of achieving results.

Capsule gun
This device (described on page 122) can produce realistic effects, again, without actual damage to the glass. This is useful where automobiles are required to have their windshields shot at.

Gelatine capsules filled with petroleum jelly are fired at the glass with sufficient force to rupture the capsule and spread the jelly across the surface. The capsules may have small black discs and pieces of tin foil added to their filling. The theory is that the black disc resembles the hole and the foil will give a better shatter effect on the glass, but success is a matter of chance.

Shatter glass
Ordinary glass may be treated to provide dramatic bullet holes but in this case, unlike the effects described above, the glass is actually smashed by the impact.

A sheet of clear, self-adhesive plastic (of the type used to cover pictures or books) is applied to a sheet of thin window glass. This must be done carefully to ensure that air bubbles are not trapped between the two materials.

Mirrors may be similarly treated, but the plastic sheet in this instance need not be clear.

To produce the bullet holes in glass treated in this fashion it is necessary to fire a projectile right through it. The capsule gun, this time loaded with steel slugs, produces an admirable effect.

A mirror can appear to be shattered by a bullet if a captive, spring-loaded bolt is released from behind. Few splinters of glass escape from the adhesive backing, but if an actor is close to the mirror, it should be fronted with a protective sheet of acrylic plastic.

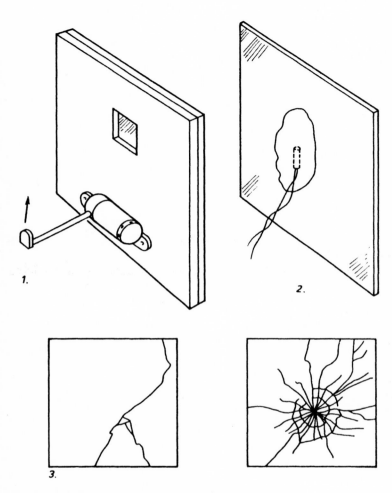

BULLET EXPLOSIONS IN GLASS AND MIRRORS

1. Mechanical method
A spring-loaded door closer can be used to smash a mirror from behind.

2. Explosive method
A mirror can be shattered by placing a bullet-hit behind it and covering the spot with a chunk of modelling clay. This method must not be used close to actors as small fragments of glass are projected with considerable force.

3. Improving the effect
Mirrors or sheets of glass that are shot at with metal projectiles (including the spring arm) will break disappointingly (*left*) unless they are covered at the back with adhesive plastic sheet. This produces a much more satisfactory visual effect (*right*).

119

Bullet Effects on People

'Walking toward the window, the man is suddenly riddled with bullets.' So might the studio directions appear in a script. But to achieve such human destruction the effects designer must employ protective devices to ensure that he does not injure the actor playing the part.

Bullet plates
These are metal plates designed to protect performers who are to be subjected to bullet hits. The plates worn under clothing, must be sufficiently thick to absorb the shock of the explosion and formed in such a way that no part of the person's body can be in line with the shrapnel effect caused by the exploding plastic case.

Bullet hits usually occur (dramatically) in the chest or shoulder and consequently the most difficult areas to protect are the underside of the face and the insides of the arms. Designs for bullet plates must take this into consideration. Usually it is wise to ensure that an overhang of the metal plate adequately shields the face, however far forward the actor inclines and that the arms are protected by costume sleeves of suitable thickness.

Blood
Bullet hits on the body must first rupture the clothing and then produce a flow of blood. To do so the bullet hit must be positioned just under the clothing. The blood comes from a rubber sac (a balloon will do) placed behind the bullet hit. It is a mistake to place the bullet hit behind the blood sac as this usually prevents the clothing from rupturing.

Operation
It is quite feasible for an actor to detonate bullet hits on his own body by having a switch secreted in some part of his clothing. This method does, however, sometimes cause the actor to react prematurely. It is generally better if the effect can be operated out of shot. Wires down the trousers terminating in a small two-pin connector can be coupled to a line on the floor.

Viewpoint
It is not easy to show both the gun being fired and the bullets striking the body in the same frame unless the gun too is wired up and fired simultaneously with the bullet hits.

A pyrofuse and black powder charge in the gun barrel suffice for a single shot.

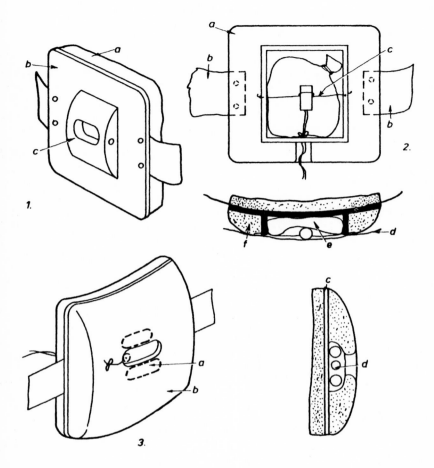

BULLET EFFECTS ON PEOPLE

1. Bullet plate
The plate is so designed that the body, particularly the underside of the chin and face, is completely shielded from flying pieces of plastic detonator. a, Plastic foam padding. b, Metal bullet plate. c, Shielded hole to accommodate bullet hit.

2. Bullet plate with large blood sac
a, Metal plate. b, Strap. c, Nylon cord. d, Actor's clothing. e, Blood sac. f, Plastic foam.

3. Alternative version
This type uses plastic foam instead of the shielded hole to trap the flying debris.
a, Blood capsules. b, Plastic foam. c, Metal plate. d, Bullet hit.

Bullet Effects Using Compressed Air

Bullet effects actuated by compressed air are often cheaper than those using wired-in pyrotechnics, but are seldom as effective.

Capsule gun

This takes many forms, but the principle involved is similar to that of the ordinary airgun. A metal barrel containing a projectile is sighted and fired at a target, the projectile being propelled by a charge of compressed air (or carbon dioxide) released through a quick-action valve.

Some of these guns have magazines permitting rapid fire while others comprise a cluster of single-shot barrels each capable of being independently sighted and fired. The magazine types are usually fired 'from the shoulder' while the others are more often rigidly positioned.

The projectiles used in these guns vary. Sometimes they are heavy metal slugs to shatter bottles, vases or mirrors while others are fragile pharmaceutical capsules designed to break on impact and scatter their contents over the area of contact. Capsules filled with powder may be used to stimulate the dust caused by a bullet striking rock while, filled with grease, they provide a passable imitation of broken glass.

It is essential to fire the capsules only at hard, inflexible surfaces, because they may pass right through soft materials.

Cycle pump

For a single bullet hit on a rock it is feasible to use an ordinary cycle pump. This may be employed in two ways. One is to bury the end of a flexible tube in a heap of powder, and the other is to suck powder into the pump and discharge it via the tube. Both will give a swift spurt of dust which, when combined with a dubbed sound effect, will look remarkably convincing.

The advantage of using this type of effect is that, unlike a bullet hit, it can be positioned very close to an actor's face.

If the operators can be hidden, cycle pumps can be used with equal effect in long shots. Fuller's earth or cement powder is invariably used for this trick.

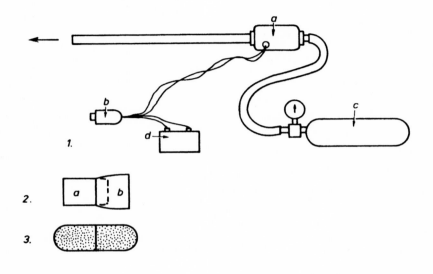

BULLET EFFECTS USING COMPRESSED AIR

1. Single barrel compressed-air gun
Also known as the capsule gun. a, Solenoid valve. b, Control button. c, Compressed air. d, Battery.

2. Metal projectile
a, Projectile. b, Skirt made from adheisve tape. The skirt expands in the barrel to form an airtight seal.

3. Gelatine capsule projectile
Both types of projectile are loaded via the barrel and pushed down with a rod. The gelatine capsule needs a wad of cotton wool behind it.

123

Safety Precautions

One of the most dangerous aspects of effects work is the use of pyrotechnics and explosives. It would seem unnecessary therefore to underline the need for suitable safeguards, but accidents sometimes occur even when all precautions appear to have been taken.

Pyrotechnic material

When working with loose pyrotechnic mixtures, ensure that all containers are closed or covered. Keep amounts to the minimums required and divide large amounts into smaller containers. Use non-ferrous implements to avoid producing sparks.

Don't store pyrotechnics that have been specially designed for particular jobs, unless their characteristics and formulae are shown on the container.

When testing experimental work do so under conditions as near to those finally envisaged as possible. What seems reasonable when fired in a sunlit, open field may be extremely dangerous at close quarters in a studio.

Wiring up

When wiring up a sequence of ground explosions, carefully mark the wires by tying sequences of knots at either end of single leads. Never connect anything to a wire without first making certain that the battery or firing box is not attached to the other end. It is not sufficient merely to disconnect one pole; somebody kicking the leads could cause reconnection.

In an uncomplicated sequence using conventional components, it is seldom necessary to test the circuit before firing, but if in doubt, use a detonator circuit tester (*never* an ordinary test meter).

Flammables

When using gasoline for fire sequences apply it from containers with nozzles. Ensure that flammable liquids are not spilled or splashed onto clothing. Keep all containers well away from the scene of fire. Ensure that fire-fighting equipment is placed at strategic places. No fire effect, however small, should be carried out without at least one extinguisher available on site.

Where garments are to be set on fire, wet blankets extinguish the blaze more effectively than conventional fire extinguishers.

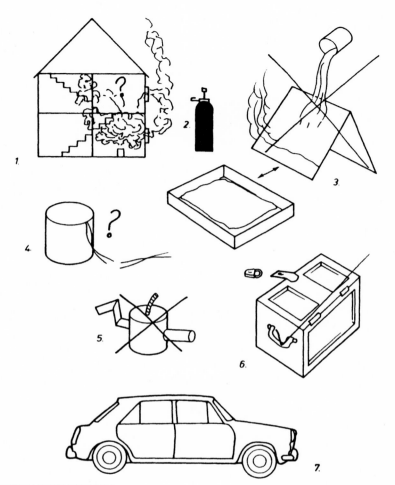

SAFETY PRECAUTIONS

1. Ensure that personnel cannot be trapped in buildings or studios before commencing fire and smoke sequences.
2. Keep fire extinguishers ready during fire sequences.
3. Don't pour liquid fuel onto something that has just been extinguished. Use pre-soaked material.
4. Always ensure that leads are not connected to firing devices before connecting explosive items.
5. Don't retain 'special' pyrotechnic items.
6. Always carry explosives and pyrotechnics in suitable containers.
7. It is usual for two people to accompany large amounts of explosives or pyrotechnics being transported by road. In the event of a breakdown one can summon help while the other remains with the vehicle.

125

Arrows

Four methods of making arrows appear to fly and to stick into their targets are given here. The techniques explained may also be applied to knives and spears.

Whip pan
This method relies upon camera work, but with suitable sound effects it can seem remarkably convincing. It also has the advantages of supreme simplicity and economy of effort.

An arrow is fixed into its target. (If human, a body-plate with a small tube to hold the arrow is required.) The camera is pointed at a position from whence the arrow is supposed to come. On 'action' the camera is panned rapidly across the scene, stopping dead when framed up on the arrow.

Flight line
An aluminium tube provided with flight-feathers is threaded onto a thin nylon line. One end of this line is fastened to the target and the other end is held taut by a length of anchored elastic. The 'arrow' may be fired along this line by a hand-held catapult or sling shot. Instead of the customary sling however, the elastic should have a small s-shaped hook which can be inserted into the end of the tube.

To prevent it bouncing back the tube must be provided with a suitable restrainer when it comes to the end of its flight. A nail fastened to the tube can be made to stick into a block of balsa wood for some set-ups, but this should not be used on an actor as a breaking nylon line would endanger him. A spring loaded trap in the clothing is sometimes used.

Spring-up arrow
An arrow fastened to a body plate and spring-loaded to fly up when released may be used to good effect. Usually this device is operated by the actor himself pulling on a nylon thread. It works well in busy scenes and where actors can spin round as the arrow flies up. It is possible to hide the arrow in the clothing. This technique may also be used where an arrow or spear is apparently shot into a tree or part of the scenery.

Reverse filming
One well-known trick is to pull an arrow out of something and by reversing the film in printing make it appear to be going in. To get a good straight snatch on the arrow it is a good idea to tie it to a light nylon line which has its other end tied to a long length of elastic.

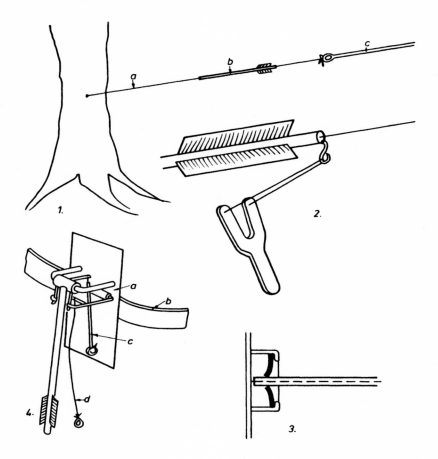

ARROWS

1. Flight line
a, Thin nylon line. b, Tubular arrow. c, Elastic rope. The tree is the target. The elastic rope holds the flight line taut.

2. Firing device
The arrow can be projected along the flight line by an ordinary catapult or sling shot with a hook to insert into the end of the tube.

3. Bounce trap
To prevent a tubular arrow from bouncing back, a simple rubber-washer trap can be set under the actor's clothing.

4. Fly-up arrow
a. Metal plate. b, Strap. c, Elastic spring. d, Release cord.

127

Knives

Knives that produce bloody wounds can be constructed in the same fashion as the dagger explained on page 130. Similarly knives that appear to have been thrown can be constructed on the principle explained for spring-up arrows on page 126.

Compressed air knife thrower
A knife with a cylindrical handle can be fired from a 'gun barrel' tube by propelling it with compressed air. It can be fired with considerable force and accuracy and may be safely used to stick a knife into woodwork within inches of an actor. Needless to say, all sensible precautions should be taken. The gun must be rigidly fixed and should be provided with an efficient sight. Correct air pressure must be determined by practice shots and maintained thereafter.

Two important factors are the length of the barrel (about 5ft is nominal) and the air release valve which should be of a type that permits full air-pressure to be applied with a minimum of delay.

Knife-throwing act
This is a board in front of which stands a beautiful circus girl while her partner throws large knives or hatchets around the perimeter of her body. In the event of there not being a skilled knife throwing artist available, the effect can be achieved by using spring-loaded knives which flip up from out of the board itself. The board, covered by a thin sheet of foam-plastic, has slits to permit free movement of the knives, the handles of which should be as thin as possible. A garish design on the board camouflages the slits.

The knives can be released by solenoid catches operated remotely.

Care must be taken that the performer does not move out of position because the knife handles can deliver a powerful blow.

Safe knives
Knives cast in latex from plaster moulds may be used for fight scenes where safety of artistes is important.

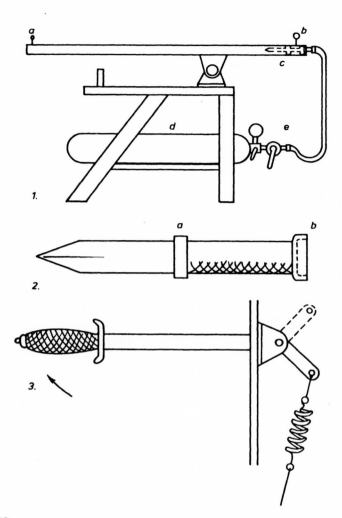

KNIVES

1. Compressed air knive thrower
a, Foresight. b, Backsight. c, Knife. d, Compressed air. e, Operating valve.

2. Knife for compressed air thrower
a, Piston washer. b, Cup washer. The scale is indicated above (1). The 'barrel' of the thrower is generally about 5ft long.

3. Spring-up knife
An alternative method is to conceal a flat dummy knife in a thin slot suitably camouflaged. A spring mechanism flips the knife upward when required.

Swords and Daggers

Property knives and daggers with retractable blades are simple to construct, but swords and rapiers present many problems. When in the course of the action these have to appear to be thrust into an actor's body it is nearly always necessary to adopt suitable camera viewpoints and sympathetic editing.

Dagger
The blade, spring-loaded to retract into the handle, should have parallel sides and a short, blunt point. This is necessary to ensure that the tip of the blade can be lost from sight in the thickness of clothing. Blood, contained in a piston in the handle can be made to flow down a tube concealed in the blade.

Fixed dagger
A shallow, slot-shaped container attached to a plate worn under clothing will receive a sawn-off dagger for scenes in which such a weapon is supposedly stuck into a human body. It is not very practical for the insertion to be undertaken as part of the action. It is better to fix the dagger beforehand and for the action to be mimed, shielded from the camera by the victim's body. Then, when he falls the implanted dagger can be seen protruding from his back.

An alternative method and one which calls for only a small hole to be made in the clothing is to fix a threaded spigot to the sawn-off blade which is screwed into a threaded boss harnessed to the body.

Retractable sword
A parallel blade, made in two parts can be constructed so that the lower half slides out of sight behind the upper half. The blade should be dark grey to disguise the join.

A flexible steel rule can be made to retract into a container fitted behind the handle and guard of a rapier, but best results are achieved on film by withdrawing the sword and reversing the action in printing.

Blood spurt
A dagger made from metal, or glass fibre and resin, can be fitted with a hollow rubber handle containing imitation blood. A fine-bore stainless-steel tube secreted in the blade allows the 'blood' to be discharged as required. This is a useful implement when the blade has to be drawn across some part of the body, leaving a bleeding gash.

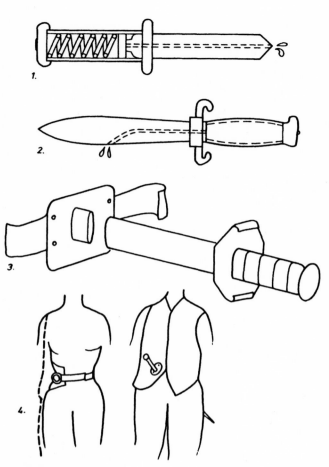

SWORD AND DAGGERS

1. Stabbing knife
The blade is retractable and the piston handle squirts 'blood' from the point of the blade.

2. Cutting knife
When the rubber handle is squeezed, 'blood' flows from the knife edge.

3. Dagger socket
Worn under the clothing, such a socket holds a sawn-off dagger.

4. Penetration tube
Body flesh can be pulled in between the rib-cage and the hip. A tube is inserted in the space and the clothing packed out around it. A sword can then be thrust through the tube.

131

Prosthetics

Prosthesis (definition): the replacing of missing parts of the body with artificial substitutes.

In the world of video and movie production the term 'prosthetics' is used to mean the application of body make-up to resemble wounds, growths, scar tissue, surgical operations and so on. It has become a specialist subject and its practitioners are artists in their own right.

Generally this work is the province of the make-up experts, but occasionally special effects and make-up need to co-operate.

Body attachments

Science fiction and horror movies often demand that human beings are shown with body deformations and unnatural additions. Characters with two heads, knotted fingers or eyes in the middle of their foreheads are almost commonplace.

Where items have to be attached to human skin much depends on the weight, the size and the use to which the item must be put.

Small devices can be affixed with gum or surgical adhesive tape, the joins being feathered with make-up or morticians' wax. Larger ones will need integral supports.

A false arm moulded in latex from a plaster cast taken from the performer's own limb can, where mutilation is required, be shown in close-up. In certain circumstances it can be fitted over the real arm.

Surgical gloves are often used as a basis on which to build claws or deformed hands, but where only a small local abnormality is required it is possible to use just a cut-off glove finger.

For half-human, half-robot characters all sorts of mechanical devices may be attached to the human body. If the edges are disguised with liquid latex and paper tissues they can be made to blend into the flesh without detection.

Dried latex can be removed without difficulty, but body hair should be shaved before application. The combination of latex and paper tissues may be utilised to cover wires (low voltage only, of course) and control cables. Faced with the problem of making a false eye move in the middle of an actor's forehead some sort of control line would need to be hidden under a false skin.

Directors should always consider cutting away to a reproduction of the original item. A latex cast of the performer's limbs or torso will look real enough – and suffer no pain. An example might be a control panel stuck to an actor's chest which in close-up could be smashed inwards with a hammer.

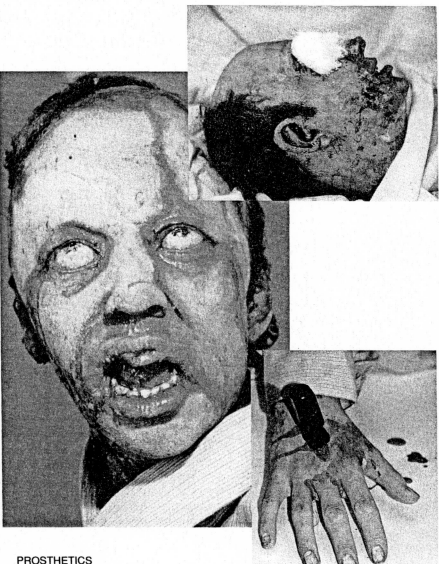

PROSTHETICS

Burns, wounds and physical injuries may be simulated by the application of various make-up materials. Paper tissues, latex and acrylic paints are invariably used to form a base over which conventional make-up is applied as a finishing or blending coat.

Supports for 'embedded' weapons can be hidden under a coating of flesh coloured latex.

These rubber models are being used to test simulated accident make-up.

133

Breaking Windows

Many effects rely more upon the manner in which they are staged than on the devices or materials themselves. Breaking windows fall very definitely into this category. Seldom can artificial glass be produced perfectly clear and yet be safe enough not to harm an actor or stunt man who has to come into contact with it. 'Soft glass' is usually thick, yellow and subject to warping while 'brittle glass' can break into dangerously sharp splinters. It is, therefore, often necessary to shoot scenes from a position where the glass cannot be seen in close detail.

Windows for jumping through
If the window is multi-paned, the framework should be constructed of ordinary lumber (it is not necessary to use balsa wood), designed in a fashion where the components lightly slot together and remain self supporting. Break-away plastic glass panes should be held in position with small blobs of putty or modelling-clay. Nails should never be used anywhere in the construction. Small wedges suffice to stiffen the framework where required.

The glass panes in the above construction smash on impact, but it is feasible to use panes of ordinary clear plastic which have been pre-broken. Providing that the window is viewed from one side or is first seen only at the moment of impact, it is not apparent that the panes are already broken. The advantage of this arrangement is that all the pieces can be reassembled and re-used.

Simulated broken windows
Unbroken windows may be dressed to look as if they are broken by applying various dressing materials. Broken plastic sheets, black paper and tin foil give the appearance of holes and jagged glass, while cracks and bullet holes can be drawn with black and white wax pencils. This strategem is used when real buildings are meant to appear derelict and enables battle and riot scenes to be filmed in street locations.

Shock wave
Where a window has to appear to break by shock or blast, it can be arranged by fitting sheets of breakaway glass into special window frames. These are provided with slotted rods which grip the bottoms of the panes of glass. When rotated by hidden levers the rods distort the glass to breaking point.

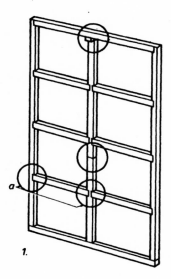

1.

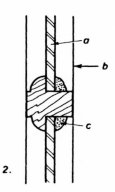

2.

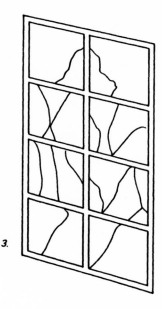

3.

BREAKING WINDOWS

1. Windows to be broken (or for stunt men to leap through) can be constructed in a way that allows them to be reassembled for re-takes. a, Glazing bar fitted very loosely.

2. Detail of window construction. a, Breaking glass. b, Direction of impact. c, Modelling clay.

3. Clear plastic resin sheet in the form of pre-broken panes can be assembled as shown. If the action is filmed and edited so that the 'glass' is seen only from the moment of impact it appears to be breaking.

Breaking Bottles, Crockery and Chairs

It is not always easy to make breakable props. If they have to be sufficiently fragile to break or come apart in the course of the action, they invariably present problems when actors have to handle them beforehand. Typical of this is a breakable chair which may have to be substantially weakened to break when smashed over the head of a performer and yet must not fall to pieces when raised in the air prior to the attack.

Bottles
Those used in fight scenes should be cast in wax. This ensures the safety of the actors and stuntmen involved.   Wax bottles are made by pouring hot paraffin wax into plaster moulds. The moulds (usually two-piece) should be free of release agents and must be soaked in cold water before the casts are taken. Once the wax has been poured in it should be quickly swilled around and the mould stood upside down to drain. This process should be repeated three times. Standing the mould upside down ensures that the wax does not settle at the bottom and produce a dangerously thick base which could cause injury. Wax bottles may be varnished for added realism.   Bottles may also be cast in plaster from flexible moulds. Such bottles are useful where they have to be thrown about or shot-up by gunfire. Bottles of plastic must be made in special moulds and it is often better to purchase them ready-made.

Cups, saucers and vases
These are frequently cast in shell-plaster, but even dry plaster does not always break as desired. It is often necessary to score items with a sharp knife beforehand.

Chairs and stools
These may be made from balsa wood or foamed rigid-plastic. The best of these is a variety of polyurethane which has a yellow colour not unlike that of wood. If balsa is used it should be selected for its softness. Some grades of balsa can be very hard and tough.

Nails and screws should never be used in the construction of breakables. Joints should be cemented.

If they are required for fight sequences, balsa wood chairs and stools should have their seats constructed from an assembly of thin sheets. Again, pre-scoring of the material assists the break-up.

Plaster
Items may be constructed from a mixture of plaster and sawdust – a useful material for props which have to crumble rather than break.

136

BREAKING BOTTLES, CROCKERY AND CHAIRS

1. Wax bottles and crockery. a, Soak plaster mould in water and drain. b, Pour in hot wax and swill. c, Invert to drain wax.

2. Balsa breakaway furniture. Use sheet wood to fabricate heavy parts.

3. Breakaway chair of plastic polyurethane foam coated thinly with plaster of paris.

4. Ornaments, statues and other breakaway items can be cast in a mixture of sawdust and plaster.

Breaking and Collapsing Scenery

The scenic designer can assist the effects designer where breaking scenery is required if suitable camouflage techniques are incorporated in the designs. (For example, large areas of plain wall are difficult to deal with.) Textured or patterned wall papers enable pre-broken areas to be disguised.

Falling shelves
Very often shelves that fall have one end fixed and the other end free. It is a simple matter to remove a peg from behind which has been hidden in the thickness of the shelf. Alternatively, if the shelf is hinged to the wall it drops forward when a retaining thread is released. This can be hidden between items on the shelf.

Brick walls
Walls can be assembled from bricks cut from expanded polystyrene. Fuller's Earth shaken on the courses of bricks as the wall is assembled provides realistic dust when it falls. These bricks are suitable for comedy programmes, but are not heavy enough to look authentic. Weighted by the insertion of lead or metal slugs and coated with liquid latex they fall more realistically but do not damage the studio floor – or such things as automobiles which may have to be driven into them.

Collapsing floor
One of the greatest problems where large areas of floor have to collapse is the fact that the weight of the floor tends to jam any release mechanism. Devices that enable the floor to be dropped easily and yet support heavy weights are shown opposite. The toggle collapses easily once it has been opened past its straight line position, but it requires a powerful initial snatch to open it. The wheeled foot is a good device if the weight has to be dropped by remote control. A solenoid-bomb release may be used to free the supporting line.

The roller is very simple and light to operate. It can be operated by a line tied to the handle, but it does require that the support is able to drop clear once it has left the roller.

Mine shaft collapse
Large pieces of expanded polystyrene covered with cloth and latex can be painted to resemble rock. Sawdust and peat adequately simulate falling earth and shale.

A breaking pit-prop can be constructed similarly to the toggle but where it has to be knocked away a small hidden wheel fitted inside the foot assists the action.

138

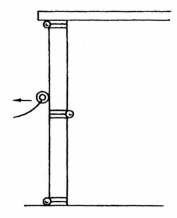

The support is 'broken' by pulling.

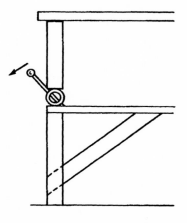

The support placed on a roller falls
away when roller is turned.

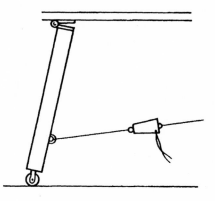

The support rolls away when the
bomb release frees the cord.

139

Lava, Quicksand and Swamps

Effects of this nature range from a person sinking slowly into the 'inexorable quicksand' to the making of footsteps in wet cement. There are basic recipes that can be adapted for many different purposes, but the techniques for their use differ widely.

Hot lava
Oatmeal, sawdust, broken cork and many other things can be used to simulate lava. Mixed with water these materials have a suitable texture, but the addition of sand adds weight when it is required for them to roll down a sloping surface.

Without 'red hot' ash and smoke they appear lifeless, but these effects have to be added independently.

Smoke may be added by pumping it into jets just ahead of the rolling lava. (It is always a wise policy to study film of the actual phenomena before trying to copy it.) In this way the smoke emulates the real thing and the jets remain free of the clogging material.

The heat can be implied either by using material which is a mixture of fluorescent-red and black ash (powdered rubber and oil) or by pouring the 'lava' over a translucent material that can be illuminated from below with orange light.

Quicksand
This is best made from a material which, when mixed with water, is light and non-enveloping. An actor plunging into a mixture of sawdust and water would be in almost as much danger as if he leapt into actual quicksand.

Quite often this effect can be achieved by floating cork chippings and cork dust on the surface of water. In this way a person can sink below the crust on the surface and swim away. Alternatively, a tank can be constructed which enables the character to raise his head under a false bank where he is able to breathe without problems, the assumption being that he has succumbed to the quicksand or swamp. An air line that can deliver bubbles to the place of immersion leads the viewer to believe that the character is breathing his last at the spot where he sank.

Swamps
Nasty swamp effects can be created by mixing water with Fuller's Earth until it has a soup-like consistency. Pieces of dry-ice thrown into this mixture not only cause it to bubble menacingly, but also produce sinister white vapour when the bubbles burst.

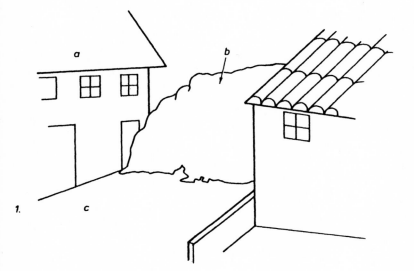

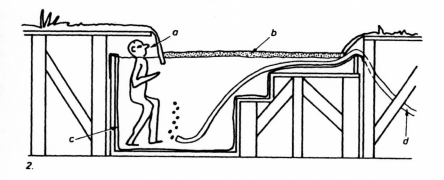

LAVA, QUICKSAND AND SWAMPS

1. Hot lava for model scenes can be created by using a heated base plate onto which is pushed a mixture of oil and sawdust. a, Model building. b, 'Lava' consisting of powdered rubber, oil and sawdust, pushed from behind. c, Heated steel plate.

2. A swamp into which an actor has to disappear can be constructed in the studio if a suitable tank or plastic lined wooden box is filled with water. The surface of the water should be covered with buoyant material such as cork granules. Where a large area of swamp is required it is usual to keep it shallow except for the spot where the man has to sink. a, Air space for actor. b, Cork and sawdust on surface. c, Heavy plastic sheet. d, Compressed air.

141

Gunge and Custard Pies

Materials used in messy scenes are invariably water-based. This makes cleaning easier and is less likely to prove objectionable to performers. The main problems arise from the use of colouring matters and dyes which in most cases are designed for their permanence.

Some of the most useful substances for gungey mixtures are the thickening agents used by the food industry. They bulk out most water-based concoctions and are generally harmless to people and props. Other materials can be used to thicken water, but these rely on their ability to soak it up, so adding bulk. Sawdust, flour and Fuller's Earth can be used for this purpose.

Oil and tar
A passable imitation of these can be made up from an intense black dye manufactured by some chemical companies. It is water-soluble and when bulked with a mixture of sawdust and alginate can resemble heavy bitumen. It is useful in that it has a low staining quality. It has been used to simulate oil-pipeline blow-outs.

Custard pies
Recipes for these are closely guarded by the circus fraternity, who regard them as trade secrets.

A quick and easy solution is to use aerosol shaving soap. This works quite well and has a good clinging factor.

Flour and water mixtures are also used, particularly where the 'custard' has to look stringy, but they are heavy and don't always stick to human flesh.

Small quantities of glycerin may be added to whipped-up soapy mixtures to sustain them and to retard drying. Machine-whipped white-of-egg (bought in quantity as albumen) produces a very light frothy mixture.

Soup
Large urns of soup may be made up from water, alginate and cocoa power with floating ingredients (carrots, etc.) cut from wine corks, but for messy eating scenes conventional tinned products, spaghetti, beans, etc. are invariably used.

Porridge oats soaked in water make a nice messy substance.

Spillages
Where gunge in the form of burnt or spilled food is required latex may be poured over saucepans, tables, ovens, etc. and allowed to dry. It can then be painted to suit and peeled off when finished with.

GUNGE AND CUSTARD PIES

Milk slopped from a saucepan or paint spilled over furniture? No problems here. A puddle of latex is poured onto a sheet of hardboard and left to dry. (The board absorbs some of the moisture and speeds up drying time.) When fully cured the puddle is sprayed with an appropriate coloured enamel paint, pulled from the board and placed wherever required. Latex can also be poured directly over non-absorbent props and stripped off after use.

143

Dirt and Decay

Although it is easy to produce scenes of untidiness and disorder it is far from easy to produce scenes which are meant to be dirty. This is because both TV and movie cameras tend to improve or beautify their subjects. To create dirty scenes it is necessary to substantially overdo the treatment.

Dust

Dust is easy. Talcum powder or cement sieved or blown over props will quickly make the point. For furniture use Fuller's Earth.

When preparing scenes in which large amounts of dust will be blown about (ceiling falls, etc.) check if studio equipment such as air-cooled cameras, computer units or precision dollies might incur damage.

Filth

For sewers, dirty cellars and similar scenes, varnish-streaked walls give an impression of seeping water, whilst sawdust, cork chips and paper thrown into puddles enhance the nastiness. Growth on walls simulated by strips of ripped polythene or sphagnum moss will complete the illusion.

Decay

Rotting wood or mouldering props can be contrived by applying mixtures of dry peat, crushed corn flakes, dyed sawdust and so on. Lentils and lichen moss stuck to items before painting give a deformed surface indicative of dry-rot.

Rotten wood to be broken in action can be pre-cast from a two-part foaming plastic (polyurethane) which is light brown in colour.

Peat

Peat is a useful material for scattering around a set to imply dirty conditions. It can be piled against walls and thrown over furniture, and is good for earth falls in tunnelling sequences.

Soot

Used in chimneys, stoves and fireplaces, black rubber dust looks exactly like soot. It can be thrown around with abandon, but not into people's eyes (it contains small amounts of abrasive materials and metal particles). It can be acquired from tyre re-tread companies, where it is ground from old covers.

DIRT AND DECAY

In a TV drama squatters had taken over this 'derelict house' and were using the battered stove to keep themselves warm. At the end of the scene the house, an inhabited cottage, was quickly restored to normal.

Cement dust, sawdust, old bricks, stips of wood, a sheet of cardboard, brick paper and a few empty packets and bottles were used to create the effect. It is invariably necessary to over-dress these sort of scenes.

Cobwebs

Artificial cobwebs placed strategically in dingy interior scenes provide an atmosphere that would be difficult to achieve in any other way. These cobwebs, usually latex-based, are sprayed from a hand-held dispenser.

Cobweb gun

Basically, the cobweb dispenser is an electric motor on the spindle of which is fitted a cylindrical reservoir containing the latex solution. It is sealed with a flat plate held in position on the spindle by an adjustable nut. The fit between the plate and the lip of the container must be good, because it is from this gap that the latex is spun in the form of threads. If the plate is screwed down too tightly no filaments emerge, whereas if the gap is too great, latex spins out in messy gobs. The fan fitted behind the container blows the latex filaments onto the set. Its blades can be constructed from thick rubber sheet or, alternatively, they may be formed of metal and protected by a suitable guard.

For convenience, some cobweb guns operate on low voltage. This means that they can be run from the power supply, via a step-down transformer, or they can be run from batteries.

Applying cobwebs

Latex cobwebs remain sticky for some time and while being applied they adhere readily to most surfaces and to themselves. Nevertheless to get them to build up in an open space it is necessary to provide some type of framework. Usually it is sufficient to string fine cotton threads across the void. In most cases these may be severed after they have done their job and allowed to go limp.

Where it is difficult to build up very large amounts of cobwebs, the work can be speeded up by using the spun plastic filaments used for Christmas decorations. These can be teased out and hung about the set.

Latex cobwebs should be dusted liberally with talcum-powder when the spraying is complete. This makes them more visible and the fall-out powder suitably complements the scene.

The mixture

Some latex preparations may be used without modification, but others have to be diluted to render them thin enough to spin properly. Care must be taken when using these substances as some are sufficiently inflammable to contravene studio fire regulations.

COBWEBS

A cobweb gun designed to be used with an electric drill.
Photo: Concept Engineering Ltd.

Wind and Blizzards

The use of a wind machine is sufficiently obvious to require no explanation here, but there are some other methods and techniques that may not be generally known.

Snow blizzard
For a studio scene in which there is a snow blizzard sequence, it is usual to set up a number of wind machines to operate in different directions. If the front one blows from right to left, the rear one should blow from left to right. This gives a richer texture than if they were blowing in the same direction.

A suitable material for driven snow is granulated expanded polystyrene fed into the air-stream in front of the blades. The effect can be augmented by smoke fed in from behind the blades (the centrifugal force of the blades widens the cloud of smoke). Where necessary solid material can be fed in from behind the blades, but this creates a sound problem. Sawdust and other similar materials should not be used to simulate snow as there is a danger that they might injure peoples' eyes.

Wind
To depict wind in the studio is often difficult as any effect is bound to be stronger near the source and correspondingly weaker further away. Sometimes high pressure air lines may be used to effect certain sequences (papers being blown about or leaves cascading along a path), but for general purposes the multi-bladed wind machine is the most useful device.

Superimposition
A glass-fronted black box can be used to provide a blizzard effect if superimposed over the main scene. Inside the box fine particles of polystyrene or paper may be whipped up into a fierce storm by using an air line or a motorised blower. The advantages of this system are that any noise can be kept away from the acting area and there is, of course, no loose material to be cleared up afterwards. This is useful in comedy shows where there is no time for involved scene changes.

Film loop
Expanded polystyrene granules blown about in front of a black background may be filmed and used later as super-imposition material for scenes in the studio where a real blizzard would be impractical. Smoke blown and filmed in the same fashion can be used to resemble a sand storm, but this is more dramatic if filmed by an 'undercranked' camera to double the speed of the action.

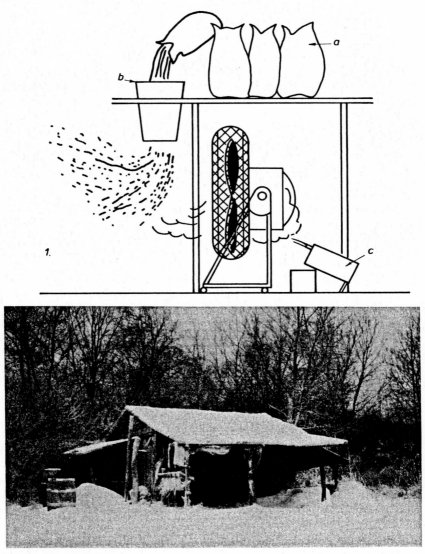

Photo: Snow Business

WIND AND BLIZZARDS

1. Set-up for sustained blizzard sequence
a, Bags of expanded polystyrene. b, Hopper. c, Smoke gun.

2. Calm before the storm
Artificial snow which when used in a controlled blizzard sequence will not blow away (see paper snow, page 152).

149

Frost and Ice

Frost
If properties or scenery are lightly wetted they can be given a coating of talc or powdered chalk blown from the palm of the hand. If a stronger bond is required, a small quantity of soluble glue can be added to the water. Aerosol sprays of 'Christmas' frost can be acquired from specialist suppliers and party shops.

For misted windows that need to be cleared in vision it is possible to spray a clear spirit mixed with talcum powder. NOTE: With most volatile spirits, there is a fire risk during spraying.

Ice
For a small area of ice on the surfaceof water (tubs, sinks, small ponds, etc.) paraffin wax may be used. The wax is melted and poured onto the surface of the water which itself must be hot. When both have cooled, the wax sets in a smooth layer similar to natural ice. It will break realistically.

For larger areas, the wax can be prepared separately in shallow trays (the smaller the depth of water the quicker the process) and floated on water where required. A square vessel is preferable to a round one because ice breaks in semi-straight lines. Thickness depends on the amount of wax used.

Very large areas (rivers and lakes) can be covered with thinly cut expanded polystyrene sheets, the upper surfaces of which may benefit from being painted (natural ice is more often grey than white).

Ice blocks
To create a block of ice it is possible to construct a credible simulation from sheets of acrylic resin (Plexiglas or Perspex) which have been heated and distorted. Welded together to form a tank and filled with water these sheets will look realistic, although size is limited. Fill through a single hole. Laid flat (a human body discovered under the ice perhaps?) the internal water pressure presents few problems. Stood upright however, the head of water may burst the lower seams. Action with this sort of prop is limited and should be avoided where weight is a factor.

There are few reasons why real ice blocks should not be used if a quick shoot can be guaranteed. Stored in a container along with dry ice their temperature can be reduced, delaying a melt down. Ice thus super-cooled should not be handled with naked hands.

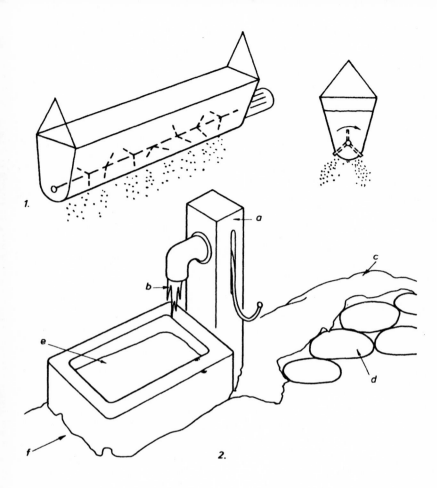

SNOW, FROST AND ICE

Ice and snow effects must usually be applied in such a way that they do not permanently damage scenery or props.

1. Snow dropping box
This motorised unit has a spiked revolving rod which distributes shredded paper through the slots in the trough.

2. Frozen prop
a, Applied frost. b, Resin icicles. c, Cloth covered in sawdust. d, Sandbags to build up drifts. e, Wax ice. f, Heaped polystyrene granules.

Snow

The two main categories of snow are falling snow and laid snow. There is also the blizzard. All three are frequently required for studio and location work.

In the studio the materials used must be non-toxic and fire resistant; outdoors the laid variety must adhere and not blow away; it must also be kind to trees and grass.

Because of its excellent visual qualities, industrial salt is sometimes used for laid snow, but should never be employed where it would corrode the wheels of camera dollies or metal-work, or where it would kill vegetation.

Certain powder-filled fire extinguishers may be sprayed around to whiten rough ground or areas of concrete or asphalt.

Fire foam generated by commercial equipment is often used to cover large areas outdoors but has a relatively short life.

Falling snow in studio

For gently falling snow, pre-shredded paper or macerated polythene is dispensed from snow machines hung above the studio set. A motor-driven spiked-rod pushes the material through slots in the bottom of a container. Outdoor paper snow cannot be used in snow machines.

Falling snow outdoors

This is best left to specialist contractors who can provide powerful blowers which blast paper snow into the air above the action. Wind machines can turn this into a blizzard, but a gentle snowfall is impractical on a windy location.

Paper snow

A technique based on interlocking paper flakes can be used for both falling and laid snow outdoors. On the ground the flakes interlock producing a stable covering unaffected by winds of up to 20 miles per hour. For even greater stability, a water spray is used to dampen the material. With this technique it is possible to apply snow to buildings and vegetation. Regarded as non-toxic, non-irritant, non-corrosive and bio-degradable, it is also fire resistant and harmless to fabrics and delicate surfaces.

Paper snow may be bought and spread by hand; for outdoor work, the equipment used for covering large areas may be hired.

Polystyrene granules
Spread on the studio floor, polystyrene granules will resemble snow. Large drifts can be simulated by laying it over sacks of sawdust or fireproofed straw. Indoors where they can be swept up polystyrene granules are popular; outdoors they blow around and are difficult to clear afterwards.

For blizzards see page 148.

Fog and Mist

To achieve the effects of fog or mist it is not always necessary to fill the studio with clouds of smoke. There are various aids to producing the desired effect, but each has its own applications and the problem should be thoroughly analysed before a method is chosen.

A foggy night
Night scenes provide better conditions than day for the simulation of fog. The dark backgrounds give greater contrast with the white swirling fog or mist and make it easier to see. Low key lighting also helps and this is more easily achieved in night scenes than in day. A moderate application of smoke behind the action gives a suitable effect if all back-lighting is switched off. A similar amount in front of the action completes the picture and as far as possible both areas should be front lit. The smoke should be passed over dry-ice to cool it and the studio ventilation system turned off for the duration of the sequence.

A foggy day
Conditions are the same as for the night sequence except that much more smoke has to be used. Lighting should be arranged so that it bounces back off the smoke rather than shines through it.

Fog filters are available for TV and film cameras.

A reasonable illusion can be created by superimposing a previously filmed fog effect – this is known as a 'fog loop' (see below).

Vignette
A vignette of white material placed in front of the lens softens the edges of the picture and by causing light to flare back into the camera creates a degraded image that augments smoke and other devices used. The effect must not be used where the camera pans around, because the treated area is then noticeable.

Superimposed effects
A reasonable illusion can be created by superimposing the effect. One of the best sources of superimposition is the fog loop. Smoke filmed against a black background can be superimposed over the main picture to give a realistic effect, but as it is slow moving it is impracticable to use the loop effect when rapid pans or cuts are necessary in the sequence. Cuts can be accepted if the final recording can be edited so that there is an appropriate 'jump' in the fog at the time of the change of viewpoint, but panning makes the fog appear to race across the picture.

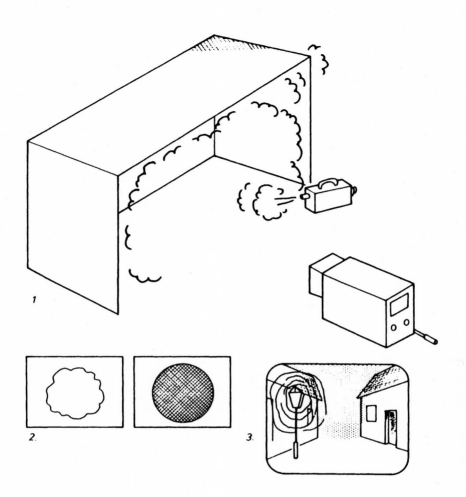

FOG AND MIST

1. Fog retainer
A light scenic construction can be erected to localise and retain smoke used for fog effects. It should have an open weave muslin roof or a plastic sheet to allow the scene to be lit.

2. Effects filters
Various filters may be used over the camera lens to soften or fog the scene.

3. Lamps for emphasis
A street lamp helps to establish the presence of fog or mist.

155

Rain in the studio

Rain, which so often interferes with location filming, can sometimes prove to be almost as great a nuisance when it is created in the studio. The problems lie not so much in producing the rain as in dealing with it when it reaches the floor.

Rain in the studio
Falling rain is usually achieved by arranging a series of drilled water-pipes over the scene below. Fixed pipes give an obviously static pattern of rain and to counteract this, alternate pipes must be gently rocked back and forth. A low-speed wind-machine, suitably positioned, adds a touch of realism.

Where long runs of tube are installed, the drilled holes nearest the supply spurt fiercely while those furthest away do little more than dribble. To overcome this, the pipes must be fed from both ends and, if necessary, also in the middle.

Rain down a window
A sheet of clear rigid plastic or glass positioned behind the studio window suffices for this effect if a length of drilled water pipe is suitably angled at the top.

If the sheet of glass is framed, a trough can be constructed in the bottom of the frame to collect the water. It is then an easy matter to install a small, electrically driven pump to return the water from the trough to the pipe at the top, allowing the effect to run continuously without supervision.

Wet/dry/wet
If practical falling rain is introduced between the camera and the actors it is not necessary for the performers to get soaking wet. This is important because rehearsals, retakes and hold-ups would cause the actor's clothing to become saturated.

Supplementary pipes behind the acting area will give depth and convince viewers that the rain extends to the back of the scene.

A pre-recorded rain loop can be superimposed over the scene but prohibits panning movements because it moves with the camera.

Water on the floor
A stout tarpaulin with its edges raised on lengths of timber is used to contain fallen water. Under this it is prudent to place layers of cloth. Sacks of sawdust should always be on hand to dam major leaks.

Where possible a sump area should be incorporated in the layout so that the water can be pumped to an outside drain.

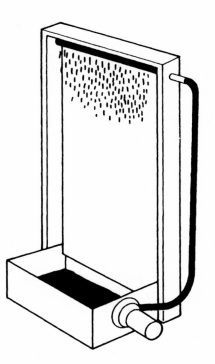

Rain on windows
Placed behind studio windows this rain effect can be left to run without attention.

Rain in the Open

Simulated rain outdoors can present problems, the principal one being that of supply. Few locations have conveniently placed hydrants, and even when water tankers are brought to the site these may have to be re-filled during the shoot.

Water tankers are heavy vehicles and sink easily into soft ground. Locations should be chosen where the tankers have ease of access and hardstanding.

The nearer to the camera it can be deployed, the more effective simulated rain will look; in wide landscapes or long shots it is quite possible for a rainfall to pass literally unseen. If a foreground object can be positioned where it will drip with water the effect will be enhanced.

Rain heads

Rain may be delivered from any types of nozzle, but the most popular is a specially designed rain head. This is fixed to the end of a metal pipe and can be hand-held and directed where required. In tracking shots it can follow the action.

For storm sequences rain heads may be moved briskly from side to side, but only a wind machine will provide the authentic impression of swirling sleet.

It is often possible to hire a local fire engine and its crew for location sequences. The standard fire-fighting branches (nozzles) produce a very adequate effect when directed upwards. Some units are equipped with water 'umbrellas' which are useful when a fine misty spray is needed.   Domestic pump-up garden sprays can be used to provide gentle rain for close-ups and, with various adaptations, will supply it in several forms. These sprays can be used to feed short runs of overhead drilled pipes. Pressurised-water fire extinguishers that can be refilled give more powerful effects.

Rivers and ponds

Locations near water are often chosen for rain sequence purposes because motor-driven pumps can be used to supply heads or nozzles. However, special filters must be employed if the equipment is to remain free of weeds or other clogging materials.

For mute takes the noise of a heavy pump may not matter, but where dialogue is required it is necessary to cover the unit with a sound suppressing blimp.

Radio Control

Radio control units used for hobbyist pursuits may be adapted to perform a number of operations, both electrical and mechanical. Heavy-duty professional units are also available commercially.

Master controls
For operations such as flying model aircraft or controlling model ships, radio control can be made to perform several functions by the use of a joystick. This is convenient where the left/right and up/down motions can be set to mimic the motions of the device being controlled. Simpler devices operate from a series of switches.

Explosions
The triggering of explosions is often carried out by the use of radio control units, but the equipment for this type of operation should be in the professional range. The use of a single frequency in the hobbyist band should never be considered, if only for the reason that it could be activated by someone using similar equipment with the same frequency.

Where the operation is of such critical importance two different frequencies should be used, each operating an individual part of the circuit or, alternatively, a coded signal.

Where, say, a distant boat or a model ship must be blown up it is more convenient to use radio control than to lay out long runs of cable. However, this can sometimes mean the non-recovery of the slave unit. The alternative is to float the receiver out-of-picture and run a firing line from that to the explosives.

The dangers implicit in wiring up explosives to a radio receiver are obvious, and sensible procedures should always be adopted. The operator whose task it is to make the connections to the slave unit should always be at a safe distance from the explosives should these fire prematurely.

Big explosions look more dramatic if two or more charges are fired in quick succession. This is easy to achieve with the rotary switch of a firing box, but when radio control is used the delay can be accomplished either by connecting the charges together with quick fuse or by employing a stepping switch pulsed from the master control unit.

Remote Control

Some effects can be operated locally (shelves and pictures can be dropped by removing nails or supports from behind). Others have to be controlled from a distance.

Electric ignition
A novel method of releasing something can be achieved by using one or more pyrofuses (page 112) and a nylon drop line.

The item to be released is tied to the nylon line, which passes through a transverse hole in a short length of metal tube. This tube has a diameter sufficient to accommodate a pyrofuse, which is positioned with its head against the line. A small plug of paper is inserted to trap the spark and retain the heat.

Firing the pyrofuse causes the nylon to melt and release the load. A priming of gunpowder is needed for heavy lines.

Solenoids
Electrically energised solenoids are useful devices for remote control, but they consume a great deal of current and have only a short operating travel. For most efficient use they should be incorporated in mechanisms where they release levers, these taking the weight or the strain. A typical example is shown for a dropping box.

Bowden cable
A stranded steel cable in an armoured sheath can be used for pulling things. For light work it will also push, but generally push/pull motions are achieved by employing a return spring. A cable of this kind can also be used for light rotational movements (the movements of dials or the hands of a clock).

Pneumatics and hydraulics
A plastic tube with a balloon fixed at either end can act as a remote-control device for certain purposes. Before being fitted, one of the balloons is inflated to its full capacity so that when released the air pressure equalises, half inflating both balloons. When one balloon is squeezed the other expands – useful for breathing dummies and pulsating nasties.

Two bicycle pumps can be connected to perform in a similar fashion. Filled with water or oil they will transmit considerable energy.

Professional air-control equipment and hydraulic systems can be purchased from commercial manufacturers or hired from theatrical property suppliers.

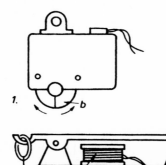

REMOTE CONTROL

Remote control devices must be simple and foolproof.
1. Bomb release type with sideways-opening jaws (b). 2. Release using lever attached to solenoid (a) to hold the heavy weight. 3. A nylon line passing between two holes in a metal tube is severed when a pyrofuse is ignited close to it. a, Nylon line. b, Metal tube. c, Plug. d, Pyrofuse.

Destruction of Automobiles

Part of the stock-in-trade of effects design is the destruction of auto mobiles. These unfortunate vehicles are blown up, burnt out, shot a and deliberately crashed.

Destruction by fire
Although the vehicle is going to be destroyed it is wise to deal with the gas tank before operations commence. It can explode dangerously i left full of vapour. The risk can be overcome by filling the tank with water.

A popular method of ignition is by electrical firing of a pyrotechnic charge placed in close proximity to a plastic bag of liquid fuel. To avoid explosion open two or more windows.

The upholstery in an automobile can smoulder for many hours and sometimes a vehicle reignites after it has been extinguished.

Exploding vehicle
Either high explosives or pyrotechnics will effectively demolish an automobile, but the latter invariably produce more smoke. Unless the scene is to be blotted out the car should be positioned down wind.

If the doors are to fly off, the hinges should be unscrewed and windows kept shut.

It sometimes happens that a windshield flies out in one piece. If it is toughened glass, but has to shatter, a bullet-hit should be placed against the glass (held there by a chunk of modelling-clay) and fired simultaneously with the explosion. To enhance the effect of an explosion on a stationary auto, remove two wheels, place the car on wooden blocks and stand the wheels back in position. The blocks can then be demolished by smaller charges.

Smoke from a travelling automobile
This is best arranged by having a smoke gun operated from inside the vehicle, but if pyrotechnic smoke is used it should be fixed to a part of the vehicle (or mounted on an outrigger) well away from the gas-tank vent.

Steam from the radiator
Use a can or stout plastic bottle that can be sealed. The cap should be provided with a quarter-inch hole.

To operate the effect, fill the can two-thirds full with hot water and add several small pieces of dry ice. Screw the cap down and position the can near the radiator. A jet of harmless 'steam' shoots up from the hole. Useful when scalded arms or faces are called for.

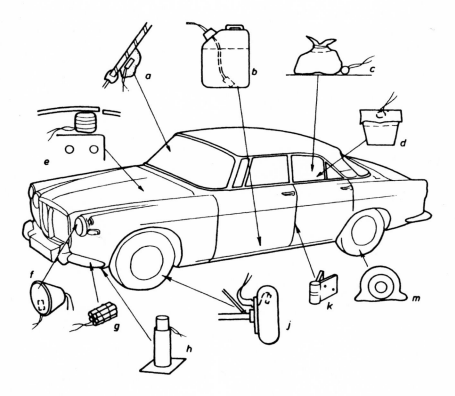

DESTRUCTION OF AUTOMOBILES

a, Bullet-hit held to windshield with block of clay. b, plastic canister, containing gasoline and sealed pyrotechnic explosive to create a big fire effect. c, smaller fire effect using plastic bag of fuel and thunderflash. d, smaller still, a plastic bucket of fuel with an igniter suspended above. e, ground-maroon will fling open bonnet lid. f, bullet effect on lamp glass using bullet-hit. g, high explosive placed under or in a car for big blow-up. h, mortar placed to one side will lift and overturn vehicle. j, bullet-hits inserted into tyre fired via slip-rings mounted inside wheel can be used while vehicle is in motion. k, hinges should have their screws removed if pyrotechnic explosion is used in vehicle. m, a tyre cast in latex can be used for comedy flat sequence.

Automobile Crashes

For reasons of continuity or economy it is sometimes necessary to record automobile crashes without damaging the vehicles involved. Like the fake punch swung by an actor at the face of another, there need be no actual contact.

The ramp
The front wheel of an automobile driven over a ramp can press down a lever which in turn will flip over some nearby object such as a lamp-post or a pile of crates.

Demolition
A similar technique enables an automobile to 'crash' into a building, apparently demolishing it. The trick is to have, say, a shed or a store front specially rigged in separate sections and a number of powerful elastic springs to pull it apart. If the entire assembly is held in place by lines terminating at the ramp these can be released by special catches as the wheel runs over them. Lightweight rubbish scattered by the car improves the illusion.

Turn-over trucks
Large or heavy vehicles which have to topple over as they speed round tight bends are invariably fitted with a special ram or mortar. This takes the form of a heavy steel tube welded to the chassis with its open end a few centimetres from the ground. It contains a wooden plunger which, on cue, is fired from the tube by gunpowder or compressed nitrogen. The plunger having nowhere to go pushes the vehicle upwards on that side.

The fitting of this type of equipment and the driving of the truck is best left to expert stunters.

Vehicle repairs
It is not unknown for vehicle crash sequences to go wrong. A mistimed cue or late braking might damage a vehicle which is needed for the retake.

Providing it can be driven, an automobile with superficial damage can be 'repaired' cosmetically by special-effects experts. Using such materials as card, plastic and expanded polystyrene it is usually feasible to build up the damaged areas to resemble the original bodywork.

1.

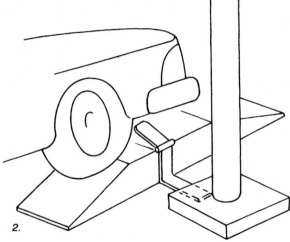

2.

AUTOMOBILE CRASHES

1. False angles
By placing bushes at an angle and setting the camera so that they appear to be upright the vehicle plunging through them will appear to be crashing on its side.

2. A jolting ramp
A specially constructed ramp containing a lever can be made to fling heavy objects away from the moving vehicle. The sudden jolt at the front of the automobile enhances the effect of a collision.

165

Special Lighting Devices

Certain items require to be specially lit if they are to be seen to advantage. Some may require illumination from behind, others from the side and yet others from the true front with no shadows. The devices described here were designed for these sort of special applications.*

Axial lighting
Positioned in front of the camera at 45 degrees to the axis of the lens a fifty-fifty mirror or even a sheet of glass will bounce light from one side on to the object being recorded. This arrangement is particularly useful where there is a need to suppress shadows. Being on the same axis as the camera lens, every shadow is directly behind the object which produces it and is therefore unseen by the camera. Crumpled paper, multi-planed cardboard animations or battered metal objects can look better in such shadowless light.

Black-spot lighting
It was discovered some years ago that certain small objects, such as a butterfly or a leaf, look more interesting if lit from behind. The snag was that a lamp in this position would be shining straight into the camera lens.

The answer was to use a 35mm slide projector containing a slide with a circular opaque mask in the centre and for this image to be focused on the camera lens. The lens in this situation sees no light while an object placed elsewhere in the projected beam is illuminated.

Eye-line
In the situation where a presenter needs to look straight at the camera lens and yet at the same time receive information from a monitor, the fifty-fifty mirror can be placed at an appropriate angle to effect this. A second mirror placed in front of the monitor will reverse the image before it is again reversed by the one between the camera and the presenter.

*For an underwater lighting device see page 30.

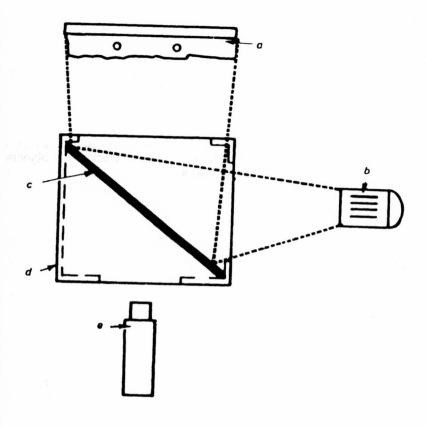

Axial lighting

A box with suitable cut-outs on three sides allows light, beamed in from one side, to travel along the axial path of the camera lens. An object illuminated in this fashion appears to have no shadows. a, Three-dimensional caption as model. b, Lamp. c, Semi-transparent mirror or sheet of glass. d, Black box. e, Camera.

167

Projected Light Effects

With the availability of computerised effects some older techniques have been discontinued along with a great deal of their cumbersome equipment. Nevertheless some of the earlier techniques still have their uses.

Static projected effects

Projectors equipped with glass slides or cut-out masks can cast light and shadows to imply that something is behind the camera, when in reality it doesn't exist. Typical would be sunlight through prison bars, open doors, stained-glass windows, etc.

Reflected light

Faced with the problem of projecting the light from a passing train onto an actor's face no electronic equipment can compete with the very simple technique of reflecting a high-powered spot on to a revolving drum of mirrors. The rectangular images flashed at a controllable rate will simulate exactly what happens in real life.

Aircraft, trains and spaceships

Scripts that call for vehicles to be travelling when in actual fact they are stationary require some sort of an effect to imply motion – windows and ports that are blank give no support to the drama.

Where software or stored effects are unavailable a source of light projected on to a revolving drum will provide all that is needed. It can be reflected straight on to translucent screens behind the windows or used in conjunction with blue-screen chroma-key techniques (page 66).

A variable-speed drum can be surfaced with different materials to give different effects. Spots of glitter can be used to simulate a space-craft passing through a meteorite shower, while a layer of metal foil which undulates will simulate the walls of a tunnel seen from an under-ground train. The same foil, lightly greased, will, when reflected on to the translucent windows of a stationary aircraft, give the impression of rushing clouds.

Animated light effects

The latest 'moving' light projectors are capable of producing a number of useful effects. Based upon a mirror system which divides a single light source into two they project the beams through rotating discs known as gobos. Their semi-three-dimensional effects include flames, clouds and water.

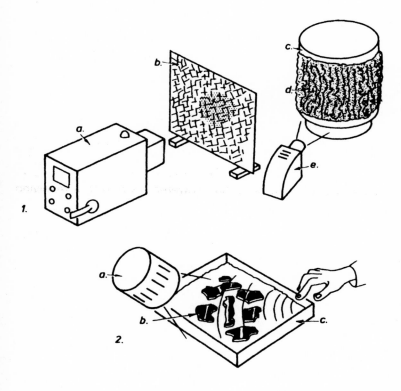

PROJECTED LIGHT EFFECTS

1. Backings for performers
Projected in this way, light can be used to provide large superimposed backings for performers appearing in front of a second camera. a, TV camera. b, Sheet of patterned glass. c, Revolving drum. d, Screwed-up aluminium foil. e, Projector light.

2. Water ripples
This set-up produces the water ripple effect associated with sea and shipboard scenes. a, Lamp. b, Pieces of broken mirror. c, Tray of water.

169

Some Special Plants

The products of horticulture and agriculture suffer severely at the hands of comedy writers. Here are some favourite gags.

Wilting flowers
A single plastic bloom fastened to a flexible tube can be made to wilt if a stiff wire, previously inserted in the tube, is slowly withdrawn from below. It is possible to reverse the action if the wire has a rounded end and the flower-stem does not kink in the wilted mode.

Falling blooms
A bloom that has to fall from a tree or plant can be electrically released if the bloom (as light as possible) is fitted with a tiny bar magnet. The branch from which it has to fall terminates in a soft-iron core (a nail will do) wound with 30 or 40 turns of insulated copper wire.

The bloom is offered up to the nail where it will remain in magnetic contact. However, when a low-voltage, high-amperage current is applied to the coil, the bloom falls. The polarity should, of course, oppose the magnet.

A reasonable number of blooms may be released in this way, but the supply leads must be of heavy-gauge copper wire.

Falling fruit
If a large number of items have to fall from a tree they can be released in the following manner: The fruit (real varieties may be used) have wire hooks inserted into their bodies. They are then hung on nylon threads secreted along the branches. The threads, passed through staples are tied off at the branch ends and at the point where they meet the trunk. They can be freed by cutting or by using a plastic detonator (bullet hit, page 112) buried under the main knot.

With this technique it is necessary to use only a few lines as each thread supports several clusters of fruit.

Leaping flowers
Sometimes a flower is required to leap from its stem. This effect can be produced by fitting the bloom with a small hollow cap which slides easily over an appropriate metal tube. Soft copper is useful here. A quick burst of compressed air causes the flower to fly off the stalk.

This system is not recommended for multiple effects unless each tube is independently fed.

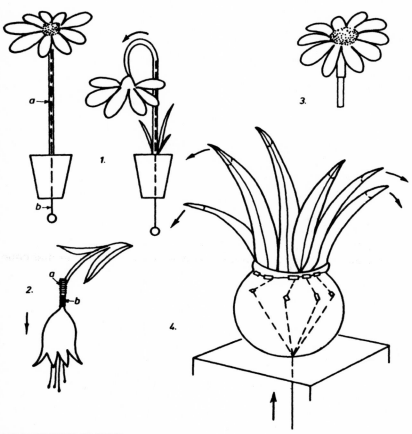

SOME SPECIAL PLANTS

Plastic blooms and leaves can generally be used, but for some effects (such as the leaping flower 3) blooms must be made from tissue paper.

1. Wilting flowers
A stiff wire in a plastic tube provides this comical effect. a, Plastic tubing. b, Stiff wire.

2. Falling bloom
Held by a magnet the bloom falls when the polarity is reserved. a, Electromagnetic. b, Magnet.

3. Leaping flower
The lightweight bloom has a hollow cap fitting over a metal tube through which compressed air can be fed.

4. Wilting Aspidistra
Operated from below with nylon line.

Modifying equipment

When hired mechanical props are required to perform in vision, they are invariably modified by effects technicians. Typical are gaming machines, coffee makers, lawn mowers, washing machines and so on. Problems are quite often encountered when these devices are wanted to operate 'normally'.

A typical example might be a gaming machine required to deliver its jackpot. Whether the old fashioned one-armed bandit or the later illuminated display machine, these devices are highly complex and to make them work on cue is by no means easy.

Cloned functions

If coins are to pour from a gaming machine it is sometimes simpler to insert a dummy chute from which coins are tipped in from behind. In some cases a close-up shot of a dummy area of the front could make the point more dramatically (and more easily), with the camera returning to the real machine knee deep in money.

A coffee dispenser (whether normal or pantomime) can be given a false nozzle which is fed from an overhead container or pressurised fire extinguisher. Washing machines that have to flood can be fed backwards through the drain hose.

Shaking equipment

If a large item, such as a washing machine, has to go violently out of control, it is sometimes a good idea to fix it to a sub-baseboard. The prop can be fastened to the baseboard by large coil springs of the type used in upholstery. The baseboard can then either be secured to the floor or held down by stage-weights.

To make the machine shudder, an electric motor fitted with a suitable gearbox and cranked arm can be used to impart the necessary oscillations. The arm should be passed through the bottom of the washing machine and connected to the baseboard.

Alternatively, the motor can be fitted with a cam in contact with a spigot that passes through the bottom of the machine.

One method of producing vibrations without any external mechanical connections is to equip the motor with an off-centre weight. Fixed to the spindle the weight produces either high speed vibrations or low speed shaking according to its size and the power of the motor.

To show an alarm clock vibrating madly as the bell goes off, the eccentric weight can be fitted to the spring mechanism.

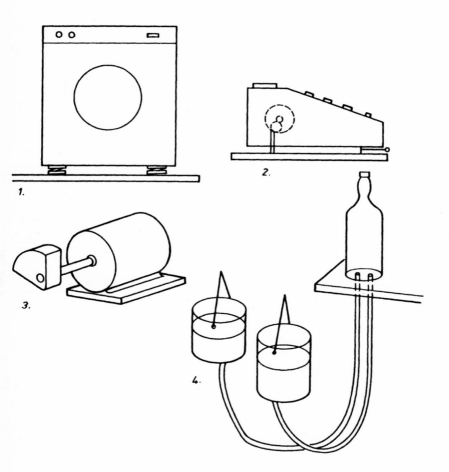

SHAKING EQUIPMENT

1. Large items that have to shake should be mounted on springs.
2. A motorised arm and crank will vibrate small items.
3. An eccentric weight on a motor shaft produces violent oscillation.
4. Two chemicals that will foam on being mixed may be introduced into a bottle by lifting the containers

173

Photographs on the Screen

In property making, model building and even costume embellishment, photographs may be used to effect substantial economies. Cut out and mounted they can be used to simulate all sorts of objects where the camera is unlikely to reveal the fact that they are only two-dimensional.

Model shots

Cut-out photographs often suffice for quick and easy miniatures. In fact they often possess a quality that the most painstaking model maker would find difficult to achieve.

For night shots the original photos should be taken in flat light to avoid give-away shadows. Where it is required to show the light coming from different directions (e.g. where the same model is being used for day and night shots or where a building is to be illuminated by flashes of lightning) small pieces of three-dimensional detail (chimney stacks, door and window surrounds, etc.) can be applied to the photograph. It is difficult and tedious to cut out around trees and bushes: It is simpler to apply small sprigs of scale foliage or tufts of steel wool or other appropriate materials.

Props

Items such as door furniture (locks, handles, etc.) can quite often be applied as photographs if the original pieces would be difficult or expensive to use. Other uses are meters and dials for such things as power-plant or aircraft-controls. The photographs if printed on light-weight paper, can be rear illuminated to resemble real instruments.

For costume work it is quite feasible to use small photographs to simulate medals, badges and even buttons. Similarly plates, ornaments, books, statuettes and all sorts of other things may be produced as photographs and displayed on shelves or in cupboards. This is particularly useful where expensive or rare items are to be used as dressing.

The photocopier

The development of the modern photocopier has given the effects designer a new and exciting tool. With its ability to reproduce coloured pictures (enlarged or reduced) without going through the normal time-consuming photographic process it offers a quick and easy means of reproduction. Magazine pictures can be used to try out backgrounds for miniatures, dials, scales, knobs and controls can all be mass produced, even picture frames for photocopied masterpieces can be constructed using nothing more than card and paste.

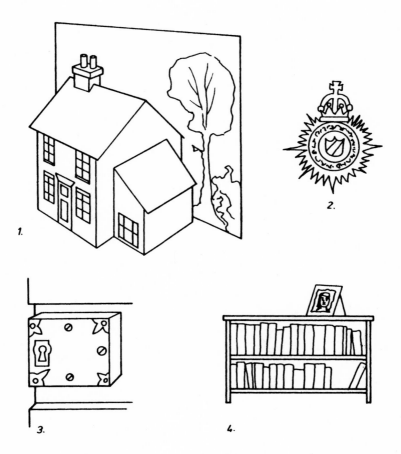

PHOTOGRAPHS ON THE SCREEN

Photographs appear to be three-dimensional on the screen because they, like everything else in the picture, are seen only as two-dimensional objects. Provided they are used with discretion they will appear as detailed objects and not merely pieces of paper.

1, Photographic background and front of model. 2, Photograph of decoration for costume work. 3, Photograph of brass lock applied to chest. 4, Photographs of books and silver picture frame.

Sparks and Flashes

Requirements for flashes range from a bolt of lightning in the sky to a flash that illuminates the scene below. Sparks occur in electrical malfunctions, safe-cutting and across huge terminals in Frankensteinian laboratories.

Because sparks suggest danger they can occasionally be used to imply something menacing. For example, a close-up of an egg in a nest would imply nothing more than an everyday object – benign and wholesome. But if that same egg were to have tiny blue sparks erupting from its shell we would presume it to be evil.

The spark coil
High-voltage spark coils manufactured for laboratory use can be employed for TV and movie effects. These coils produce bright blue sparks across their terminals (as much as 6in (152mm) apart) which, when superimposed over the main picture, can look highly dramatic.

Discharged between different shaped electrodes the sparks can be made to produce different patterns. One example is a circular cathode with a central anode. This produces a random pattern of sparks radiating like the spokes of a wheel.

Practical sparks such as these must be recorded in front of a black background. If a number of them are pre-recorded and superimposed over each other, complex interacting patterns can be built up.

Computer-enhanced sparks can be fattened and their colours altered. Computer graphics will also produce those crackling arcs that travel slowly up sci-fi electrical installations.

The scissors
The scissors, a device used by studio electricians, comprises two wooden handles hinged in the middle. At their ends they have carbon rods which, when brought together, induce an intensely bright arc. Scissors are used to simulate lightning flashes and night-time battlefield effects.

On a smaller scale an electric arc welder will produce a repertoire of sparks and flashes. A hacksaw blade connected to one lead drawn across a metal strip connected to the other will produce a shower of bright sparks.

Video camera damage
It is easy to assume that very bright light could damage a video camera, but this is not necessarily so. Most video cameras have at some time been inadvertently pointed at the sun without ill effect and there is little evidence that filming a welder at work has caused damage. If in doubt, check with the manufacturer.

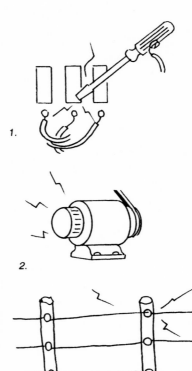

SPARKS AND FLASHES

A welding transformer can be coupled up to various props which need to spark intermittently.

1. A screwdriver connected to one terminal of the welder can be thrust into switchgear connected to the other terminal.
2. An electic motor can be wired to a welder so that sparks come from the casing when the motor is rotated.
3. An electrified fence can be seen to be alive when the wires are moved.

177

Scoring Devices and Game Shows

Because the scoring devices and visual displays associated with game shows become ever more sophisticated there is little need these days to construct anything more than the desks or stands to put them in. The range of indicators installed in sports stadia, railway stations, airport lounges and so on ensures that almost any type of display can be obtained from specialist contractors.

The visual display unit
The VDU or television monitor is now a commonplace item and can be used to relay information from the control area to the contestants' desks. Used as an indicator to be seen by the audience it can display scores fed to it from a computer or from a slave camera looking at some specially constructed game-board device.

The advantage of using a VDU is that its input can be fed into the transmission circuit and shown as a close-up picture. Furthermore it can display alternative material (such as the name of the show) while the scores aren't being used.

Slide projectors
The complex arrangements of some game-boards call for extraordinary set-ups to display the information. Several popular programmes use whole banks of slide projectors focused on to screens that are relayed by fixed cameras. Such arrangements are necessary where chequer-board patterns change colours or give different information within the same areas. The automatic slide-changing mechanism can be used to switch the lights.

Computer generation
Computer-generated patterns for game-boards allow all sorts of designs and animations to be screened. Fed into the transmission network they can fill the screen, but occasionally the limiting size of the TV monitor makes it too small to be used on the set itself. In such circumstances there could be two solutions. One would be to use an area of blue screen for chroma-key insertion (although this will not be seen either by the competitors or the studio audience), while another would be to use an Eideophor projector to furnish a much bigger picture.

Personal Equipment

Many different tools and pieces of equipment are employed in the creation of special effects, but for reasons of reliability and safety certain items are best kept in the custody of their users. This applies particularly to climbing ropes, underwater diving equipment and anything else which may be used only infrequently.

The viewfinder
The optical viewfinder is an aid to picture composition. It is a hand-held device which operates in much the same way as a zoom lens and is particularly useful when constructing a miniature in the workshop or setting a scene on location. In the studio it can prove useful when cameras and monitors are switched off.

Firing box
This item, which is used to fire pyrotechnics and explosives, is invariably designed and maintained by its user – a precaution against accidents (see page 100).

The pocket knife
Few effects operators would dream of going anywhere without a good 'Swiss Army' type pocket-knife. This essential device includes such useful components as a screwdriver, a tin-opener, a corkscrew, a small saw and a spike. With such accoutrements, effects operators can cope with most unforeseen problems or emergencies.

The electric test meter
A meter to test electrical continuity, voltage and resistance is another important item. Unfortunately it can all too often suffer accidental damage. Set at the wrong range, dropped on the floor or subjected to water and dirt on location, the test meter needs to be as rugged as possible. It is generally better to buy a cheap and simple meter rather than an expensive one with sophisticated facilities which might never be used. Some sort of protective casing will prolong its life.

The tool holder
Workers in all trades and crafts tend to carry their equipment in metal tool boxes, but there are times when something more specialised is needed. A purpose-made tool belt and material holder enables its owner to have essential items immediately to hand when engaged in complicated operations.

Further Reading

Many specialist books have limited print runs and once sold out are seldom re-issued. Anyone wishing to acquire a reference library is advised to hunt through the used book shops where many out-of-date text books can be found. Because special effects embrace so many esoteric arts and crafts, old books on subjects as diverse as taxidermy, electrical experiments and basic metalwork could prove invaluable.

Some of the books listed here may no longer be in print.

ANIMATION
Halas, J., 'The contemporary animator', Focal Press, 1990.
Hayward, S., 'Computers for animation', Focal Press.
Perisic, Z., 'The animation stand: rostrum camera operations', Focal Press.
Whitaker and Halas, J., 'Timing for animation', Focal Press.

AUDIO-VISUAL
Robertson, I., Audio-Visual Equipment: A Technician's and User's Handbook, Butterworth-Heinemann.
Simpson, R.S., 'Effective audio visual: a user's handbook', Focal Press.

ELECTRICITY
'Basic electricity (Pts 1 to 5)', Technical Press.
Bryant, D., 'Teach yourself electricity', Hodder & Stoughton, London, England.

ELECTRONIC FILM MAKING
Obanian, T.A. and Phillips, M.E., 'Digital film making', Focal Press.

EXPLOSIVES
Literature obtainable from ICI UK Ltd., Infopoint, London, England.

MAKE-UP
Baygan, L., 'Techniques of three dimensional make-up', Watson-Guptill.
Kehoe, V., 'The technique of the professional make-up artist', Focal Press.
'Special make-up effects', Focal Press.

OPTICAL EFFECTS
Perisic, Z., 'Special optical effects', Focal Press.

PROPERTIES
Kenton, W., 'Stage properties and how to make them', A. & C. Black.

PYROTECHNICS
'Unwin's catalogue', Unwin Pyrotechnics Ltd, Slough SL3 8QA, England.

SCULPTURE
Midgely, B., 'Complete guide to sculpture', Apple Press.
Lucchesi, B., 'Modelling the head in clay', Watson-Gupthill.
Lanteri, E., 'Modelling and sculpturing animals', Dover Publications.

SOUND EFFECTS
Mott, R.L., 'Sound effects, radio, TV & film', Focal Press.

SPECIAL EFFECTS
Caruso, J. and Arthur, M., 'Video lighting & special effects', Prentice-Hall.
Fielding, R., 'The technique of special effects cinematography', Focal Press.
McCarthy, R.E., 'The secrets of Hollywood special effects', Focal Press.
Wilkie, B., 'The technique of special effects in television', Focal Press.

STAGING AND SCENIC DESIGN
Byrne, T., 'Production design for television', Focal Press.
Millerson, G., 'TV scenic design handbook', Focal Press.
'Video production handbook', Focal Press.

TELEVISION OPERATIONS
Oringel, R., 'Television operations handbook', Focal Press.

TV COMMERCIALS
Gradus, B., 'Directing: the television commercial', Focal Press.

TV LIGHTING
Millerson, G., 'The technique of lighting for TV and film', Focal Press.
'Lighting for video', Focal Press.

WEAPONS
'Weapons: an international encyclopaedia - 5000 BC-2000 AD', Diagram Group.
Hogg I.V., 'Military pistols and revolvers', Arms and Armour Press.
'Military small arms', Arms and Armour Press.
Elwell, C., 'Modern American small arms', Hamlyn.

Glossary

Acrylic plastic The transparent, rigid plastic known as Perspex or Plexiglas.

Animation Stand (16) Another name for a rostrum camera.

Asbestos Since the prohibition of certain types of asbestos for industrial use substitutes have had to be found for special effects work. These replacements include rock wool, fibreglass matting and glass filament rope.

AutoFocus (26) Modern camcorders have an automatic focusing system which homes in on the subject nearest the camera – this can prejudice glass shots, fog and smoke sequences.

Beam-Splitter A semi-transparent sheet of optical glass that diverts some of the light that would normally pass through it.

Blaster (80) An imaginary hand-held weapon popularised in science fiction.

Blue Screen (66) The blue screen used for chroma-key insertion. The term 'blue screen process' is occasionally used instead of chroma key or CSO.

Bomb Release (138) A solenoid-operated hook for releasing heavy weights or cables under tension.

Bowden Cable (82, 160) A flexible stranded steel cable in an outer sheath. Used for automobile brakes and aircraft controls, etc.

Breakaway Glass (134) Plastic material used to imitate window glass where it has to be smashed. Made by pouring heated plastic onto metal sheets.

Bullet Hit (112) Plastic-cased detonator used to simulate a bullet striking its target. Electrically fired.

Case Mould (40) A flexible mould in two or more pieces backed with a rigid case to prevent it deforming.

Cel (16) Transparent plastic film on which is painted the pictures used in filmed animations.

Charcoal Tablet (86) Small circular tablets of compressed charcoal used for the burning of incense or for fuelling portable cooking stoves. Often impregnated with chemicals to facilitate lighting.

Chip (20) A miniaturised encapsulated circuit found in all modern electronic devices. It forms the basis of the computer, but can be found in many other things including electric drills, telephones, calculators, watches and so on.

Chroma Key (53, 66) An electronic method of combining parts of television pictures received from separate cameras or other sources. Used chiefly for putting backgrounds behind action. Also known as colour separation overlay.

Clone (172) a copy of anything which has been produced to faithfully resemble an original.

Cobweb Gun (146) Hand-held dispenser of latex 'cobweb' filaments.

Colour Separation Overlay (66) See Chroma Key.

Crab (54) Term used to describe camera movement when the dolly or pedestal is moved sideways.

Deflagration (98) The explosive effect of burning gunpowder.

Depth of field (26) The front to back area of a subject which is in focus when seen through the camera lens.

Detonation (98) The shock effect which causes the explosion of high-explosive materials.

Dolly (54) A wheeled truck on which cameras are mounted. Has steering and a moving arm which raises and lowers camera.

Dry Ice (74) Frozen carbon-dioxide gas in solid form. Used commercially for cold storage. When mixed with hot water generates large quantities of water vapour in form of heavy mist.

Dry-Ice Generator (74) A box or vessel designed to liberate dry-ice mist under controlled conditions.

Expanded Polystyrene (32) Attenuated, lightweight, rigid-foam, plastic material principally used for thermal insulation and packaging. Has many uses in the making of film and TV props.

Fade Term used to describe the effect where picture fades into black. Cross-fade implies that as one picture fades down another fades up to take its place.

Fifty-fifty Mirror (26, 64) A mirror which has been only partially silvered or aluminised on one surface. Used for beam-splitting or super-imposition effects.

Film Loop (148, 154) Term derived from the days when an endless loop of film was run through a back-projection machine or telecine equipment to provide a continuously running effect. Frequently used for rain, snow, fog and blizzard effects, but now as a conventional reel of film.

Flame Ark (92) Pitched-roof-shaped wire-netting frame on which impregnated cloth is burnt to provide high flames.

Flame Drum (88) Motorised, transparent-plastic cylinder on which can be painted designs to throw shadows. Particularly useful for the simulation of leaping flames.

Flame fork (88, 90) Trident-shaped pipe for the burning of gas during fire sequences in the studio.

Flash Pot (102,110) Cardboard carton containing pyrotechnic flash-powder for 'wizard' appearances and other flash effects in the studio. Usually electrically fired.

183

Frame (12) This is the outer confines of the TV picture or a camera viewfinder.

Front-Axial Projection (64) (also called AXIAL-FRONT PROJECTION). A system of projecting photographs from a point near the camera to give large background scenes in the studio.

Fuller's Earth This is a form of powdered yellow clay. It is a benign powder with many uses in special effects. It is relatively heavy and does not stay suspended in the air.

Gimbal (82) A support which allows the object supported to be rotated in any direction.

Glass Fibre (46) Fine filaments of drawn glass having very high tensile strength. Used in conjunction with polyester resin to produce the material commonly called fibreglass. Used in this form to make lightweight scenery and property items.

Glass Shot (48) A sheet of glass positioned between the camera and the scene can have part of the scene painted on it to extend the picture.

Hanging Miniature (53) A miniature used to augment the picture.

Heat Exchanger (84) A device which transfers heat from gas or liquid to similar materials of a lower temperature.

Inlay (48) Electronic method of combining part of one television picture with another. As the system requires the use of a cut out mask to define the area inlaid, the subject material must have finite edges.

Joystick (159) An operating lever that moves in different directions – left, right, forwards and backwards, etc.

Latex Latex is natural rubber which can be re-constituted in different ways. It can be made to mix with water or with spirits. It can be cured to dry hard or be allowed to dry naturally and remain flexible. It can be mixed with various fillers.

Lay-Up (46) Term used to describe the laminating of glass fibre and polyester resin.

Lichen Moss (58) A natural moss found on rocky soil in sub-arctic countries. Softens in water. Used extensively in architectural and landscape model making.

Maroon (106) A large explosive firework used to simulate the effects of shellfire. Also called a Ground Maroon.

Matte Line (56, 58) The join between parts of the picture where each part comes from a different source.

Miniature (50) A model designed to look like a real scene.

184

Morphing (22) A computer technique which changes (or metamorphoses) one subject into another without using superimposition.

Mortar (106) A steel or heavy cardboard tube used to fire objects into the air.

Mortar or Mortar Pan (106) The heavy metal pan used for firing ground maroons and bomb simulators. Because it has a similar function to the tube mortar it has the same name.

Motion Control (20) A method of storing camera movement details in an electronic memory in order that they can be repeated automatically.

Overlay (48) An electronic method of combining part of one television picture with another. Able to handle moving subjects in infinite arrangements. Uses black and white as triggering factors instead of the colour separation principle associated with colour separation overlay or chroma key.

Pan Term used to describe camera movement where it is swung to either side.

Paper Snow (152) Snow used in overhead dispensers is sometimes made of macerated paper – so too is snow used for ground dressing. The two are **not** interchangeable.

Pedestal Wheeled mounting for TV camera. Camera raised and lowered on a central column.

Periscope (30) An arrangement of two mirrors which allows a higher or lower viewpoint to be obtained. Shots very close to the studio floor can be taken by a camera fitted with a periscope.

Perspex British brand-name for clear acrylic resin.

Photocopier (174) An office machine for copying documents. Modern equipment which can reproduce in colour has several applications in effects work.

Piece Mould (40) A mould constructed in two or more pieces to facilitate the removal of the cast.

Plexiglass American brand-name for clear acrylic resin.

Polyester Resin (46) Resinous compound that when mixed with reagents hardens and solidifies. Used both for casting purposes and for the bonding of glass fibre lay-ups.

Pyrofuse (112) A small electrical fuse designed for the ignition of pyrotechnic materials.

Pyrotechnics (102) Fireworks, rockets, flares, thunderflashes, etc., containing powdered materials which burn or explode when ignited.

Reflex Screen (64) Glass-beaded material supplied in the form of sheets or rolls can be applied to a backing or to a studio wall to form a projection screen. Known as a reflex screen it reflects almost all the light that hits it back to the point from which it came. This characteris-

tic is the basis of the front-axial projection system.
Release Agent (36, 46) Substance applied to the surface of moulds to prevent adhesion of the casting compounds.
Rostrum (Animated Screen) Camera (16) A fixed movie camera mounted vertically above a work table. The camera, able to record one frame at a time, is used for film animation purposes.

Scenic Projection (64) The system of projecting large photographic images onto screens placed at the rear of the scene. A convenient method of providing realistic backings.
Slave Unit (159) Every radio control system has a master unit controlled by the operator which feeds one or more slave units that perform the distant tasks.
Smoke Gun (84) (or **Smoke Machine**) Portable machine to be carried in the hand or placed on the studio floor for the purpose of furnishing controlled amounts of smoke. Smoke is generated by the heating of oil.
Smoke Pot (86) Pyrotechnic smoke maker.
Snorkel (30) This is a term normally associated with the air-pipe used for underwater swimming. In filming it is applied to special lenses which are housed in tubes.
Solenoid (160) An electromagnetic device which imparts a limited movement to a steel core or armature.
Stop Frame (18) The process of filming something a frame at a time for animation purposes.

Telecine Machine Equipment used to transmit movie film in the form of television pictures.
Thermoplastic (34) A material which softens when heated.
Tilt Term used to describe camera movement when it is tipped up or down.
Track Term used to describe camera movement when the dolly or pedestal is moved towards or away from the scene.

Vacuum Forming (34) The method of sucking a heated sheet of plastic over a master item to reproduce its shape.

Whoofer (108) A compressed-air cylinder used to discharge pieces of material and dust into the air to resemble an explosion.

Zooming (20) The act of moving in and out of a picture by simply altering the characteristics of the camera lens.